Vintage Diesel Power

by Brian Solomon

Voyageur Press

First published in 2010 by MBI Publishing Company LLC and Voyageur Press, an imprint of MBI Publishing Company, 400 First Avenue North, Suite 300, Minneapolis, MN 55401 USA

MBI Publishing Company titles are also available at discounts in bulk quantity for industrial or sales-promotional use. For details write to Special Sales Manager at MBI Publishing Company, 400 First Avenue North, Suite 300, Minneapolis, MN 55401 USA.

Library of Congress Cataloging-in-Publication Data

Solomon, Brian, 1966-
  Vintage diesel power / Brian Solomon.
     p. cm.
  Includes bibliographical references and index.
  ISBN 978-0-7603-3795-0 (sb : alk. paper)
  1. Diesel locomotives–North America. I. Title.
  TJ619.4.N6S654 2010
  625.26'6–dc22
                              2009052066

Front Cover: In June 1961, pristine Canadian National FP9 and a B-unit catch the sun at Burk's Falls, Ontario, with train No. 41 running from Toronto to North Bay. Notice the steam-era bell mounted on the roof. *Richard Jay Solomon*

Frontispiece: On August 31, 1988, former Central Vermont No. 3604, owned by Genesee Valley Transportation, is seen at Rochester & Southern's Brooks Avenue Yard in Rochester, New York. The 1,800-horsepower RS-11 represented a significant design departure from the Alco-GE model RS-3 that it replaced. *Brian Solomon*

Title pages: At 5:00 p.m., on January 14, 1994, Burlington Northern veteran SD9 No. 6117 drills freight cars in the Northtown Yards at 35th Avenue in Minneapolis, Minnesota. Before wind-chill calculations, the temperature measured well below zero. *Brian Solomon*

Editor: Dennis Pernu
Design Manager: LeAnn Kuhlmann
Designer: Jennie Tischler

Printed in China

Contents

Acknowledgments

Years of locomotive observation, study, and research have contributed to the production of this book. It is not my first effort, and undoubtedly won't be my last, but in this book I've tried to distill and portray vintage diesel locomotives built in the 30 years following World War II. These are the locomotives that my father photographed in the 1950s and 1960s and that I grew up with in the 1970s and 1980s. Some were common, ordinary machines that functioned as the backbone of the railroad; others were oddballs, or stragglers from another era.

I owe my early interest in railways and locomotives to my father, Richard Jay Solomon, who handed me my first cameras and brought me on my first railroad trips. He has contributed generously to this effort, and many of his photographs appear here. Bob Buck of Tucker's Hobbies in Warren, Massachusetts, has likewise encouraged me for many years. Bob's interest in locomotives stems from experiencing steam and diesel power on the Boston & Albany route, and he has always conveyed his knowledge to me with enthusiasm and accuracy. Bob has lent me some his excellent period work for this book, as has his son, Kenneth. My old friends, Tom M. Hoover and his son Tom S. Hoover, are serious students of diesel engines and diesel locomotive design. Both have shared their interest and educated me on the details of American diesel locomotives. Doug Eisele of Genesee Valley Transportation is another old friend who inspired my interest in railroads in western New York State, facilitated arrangements on the GVT railroads, and contributed photographs, while helping with captions and research. John Gruber and Dick Gruber aided my interest and photography in more ways than I can articulate. They have traveled with me on various occasions to make photographs of unusual diesels and were especially helpful in matters relating to Wisconsin & Southern, and introducing me to former Milwaukee Road employees.

Thanks are owed and given to the many generous fellow photographers, railway employees, and railway enthusiasts who over the years have aided my quests for photographs and information: Norman Yellin, John Peters, Dan Howard, Doug Moore, and the late John Conn were among the many fellow enthusiasts who I accompanied on my early railroad adventures; J. D. Schmid pointed the way in regard to photography on Southern Pacific and elucidated the subtleties and significance of EMD's 20-645E3; Brian L. Jennison has traveled with me in California, Oregon, New England, and elsewhere, sharing his railroad knowledge and helping with photography; Pat Yough has traveled with me on many occasions, assisted with arrangements, and helped track down details for captions; Tim Doherty for trips in New England, Canada, and New York State; George and Candy Pitarys for marathon adventures in pursuit of antique diesels in America and Canada; Bill Linley for visits in Quebec and Nova Scotia; Mike Gardner for adventures in Pennsylvania and New England; Steve Carlson for trips on New England Central; Neal Gage for trips photographing Alcos and F-units in Maine; Don Marson for insight on matters relating to the Santa Fe and trips in the Midwest; Chris Guss for tracking down details and for insightful photographic discussions, as well as trips in the Midwest; the late Mike Abalos for intensive photographic adventures in Chicago; Sean Graham-White for organizing a memorable trip to Chicago's Clearing Yard; Chris Southwell for helping photograph the Western New York & Pennsylvania; Otto Vondrak for organizing a trip to photograph the Battenkill Railroad; Marshall W. Beecher for trips in Chicago and on Wisconsin Central; Mike and Tom Danneman for trips in Wisconsin and Illinois; Dean Sauvola for trips on Wisconsin Central; Mel Patrick for visits in Colorado; GVT's Matt Wronski for discussion of Alco diesels; Phil Brahms and Justin Tognetti for recent trips in California and Nevada; Kurt Bell for visits to the Strasburg Rail Road and Railroad Museum of Pennsylvania; David Hegarty, Denis McCabe, Ken Fox, Noel Enright, Eamon Jones, Mark Hodge, Colm O'Callaghan, John Cleary, and the many members of the Irish Railway Record Society for helping me experience vintage EMD diesels in Ireland.

Special thanks to Chris Guss, George W. Kowanski, Bob Morris, Jim Shaughnessy, Bill Vigrass, and Jay Williams for contributing images to make this a better book. To my brother Seán Solomon for traveling with me on occasion and for hosting me on visits to Chicago, Minneapolis, and Philadelphia. To my mother, Maureen Solomon, who has taken a keen interest in my photography, sometimes seeing details in photographs that I may have missed. Finally, this book would be just loose photographs and words if it wasn't for my editor Dennis Pernu and everyone at Voyageur Press for making a conceptual item tangible.

Many sources have been tapped in researching details for the introductions and captions. I've included a detailed bibliography at the end of the book. Although this is a completed volume, the research and photography are ongoing. I've made an effort to select photographs that work together, while trying to weave themes of interest into the captions. Please enjoy!

Introduction

Introduction

Dieselization was the most complete and profound change undertaken by American railroading during the mid-twentieth century. To the casual observer, the diesel appears to emerge from the depths of the Depression and bring about an unprecedented motive power revolution in just a few years' time. Most railroads made the transition from steam operations to diesel in a little more than a decade. While there were very few diesels before World War II, during the war they proved their worthiness, and after the war, American railroads embraced rapid large-scale dieselization.

However, diesel *development* was not a sudden process. The success of the diesel locomotive was the result of a blending of internal combustion and electrical technologies made possible by significant technological advances in both areas. American railroads had been familiar with the benefits of electric operations since the first decade of the twentieth century. Electric motors offered better traction characteristics and required far less maintenance than steam power. Electric locomotives enabled greater labor productivity as they made it possible to operate two or more locomotives from a single throttle using multiple-unit connections. The downside of electric locomotives was enormous initial cost of railway electrification.

Parallel with electric railway developments was that of lightweight gasoline-powered railcars colloquially known as doodlebugs. These self-propelled cars were popular in the first decades of the twentieth century for branch-line services. Key to the success of gas-electric cars was matching engine output with the characteristics of the electrical system.

The diesel-electric offered railroads most of the advantages of electric locomotives but without the high cost of electric infrastructure. In the late 1920s and early 1930s, at request of the navy, engine companies embarked on intensive development of compact, lightweight, and mostly high-output diesel engines for marine applications. Key advances to diesel engine design were made possible by the combination of metallurgical improvements, invention of better forms of high-pressure fuel injection, and new manufacturing techniques. Reliable, compact, high-output diesels proved the missing link in the design of powerful diesel-electric locomotives capable of equaling the power potential offered by state-of-the-art steam designs.

During the 1930s, several manufacturers offered diesel switchers. Although experimental road diesels had been tested in the 1920s, the first commercial road-service diesel power was developed by General Motors' Electro-Motive Corporation (later Electro-Motive Division). Following successful production of high-speed power cars for streamliners in the mid-1930s, Electro-Motive developed and perfected the first commercially mass-produced high-horsepower road diesels. This would soon change the face of American railroading. The established locomotive manufacturers, Alco and Baldwin, recognized the potential of Electro-Motive's technology but lagged behind in development and refinement of their own road diesels. Despite the promise of Electro-Motive's diesels, most railroads remained loyal to steam power as they waited to see how the new technology would fare in the harsh environment of railroad road service.

World War II intervened in the development and acceptance of diesel power by imposing complex multifaceted effects on locomotive evolution and application.

The war accelerated the development and refinement process, while temporarily stifling sales of new locomotives and simultaneously pushing railroads and existing locomotive fleets to their practical limits. Wartime traffic proved a high-water mark for traffic moving over American rails. As the war drew to a close, American railroads had a voracious demand for new power. Having experienced the benefits of diesel-electrics during the pressurized wartime traffic environment, railroads were convinced to make the enormous investment in diesel technology.

Although diesel locomotives required higher initial investment, they offered the potential for greater availability, higher reliability, lower maintenance costs, and substantially lower operating costs than steam power. After the war, only a few railroads clung to steam.

Electro-Motive had the advantage in the road-diesel market. After the war, Electro-Motive quickly established its reputation as America's foremost diesel manufacturer. The other builders followed its lead, largely emulating the styles and types of locomotives built by Electro-Motive. Alco and GE initially worked as partners. Railway supplier and diesel engine manufacturer Fairbanks-Morse entered the large locomotive market, viewing diesel locomotives as a logical application for its powerful opposed-piston engine.

Previous pages:
The first decades of American dieselization produced the greatest variety of locomotives. In March 1967 at Central Railroad of New Jersey's Jersey City locomotive terminal, we find CNJ Fairbanks-Morse Train-Master No. 2412, CNJ F-M H-15-44 No. 1502, Reading Company Alco C-430 No. 5211, and Baltimore & Ohio Electro-Motive F7s. Although diesels had ruled for more than a decade, the steam-age coaling tower was still standing. *George W. Kowanski*

A pair of Southern Pacific SD9s leads the Grants Pass Turn en route from Medford to Grants Pass, Oregon, at Ray Gold on the Siskiyou Line in May 1990. SP's SD9s were known as "Cadillacs" because of the smooth ride afforded by a six-motor Flexicoil truck. For more than three decades, the SD9s were standard power on SP's Oregon branch lines and secondary routes. *Brian Solomon*

In the decade that followed the war, American railroads largely replaced their steam fleets, leading to brisk diesel sales. Electro-Motive grabbed the largest market share. By the mid-1950s, as railroads approached total dieselization, orders began to taper off, which contributed to a shake-out in the industry. Of the big four, Baldwin slipped from third to fourth in the early 1950s and then abandoned locomotive building altogether in 1956. F-M ceased domestic locomotive production in the mid-1950s, although it continued to sell a few locomotives for export into the early 1960s. Alco and GE ended their partnership in 1953, and a few years later GE reentered the market on its own in competition with Electro-Motive and Alco.

By 1960, steam was finished, and railroads looked to start replacing World War II–era diesels with new, more powerful models. Improved designs had substantially increased both output and reliability. The builders sold the concept of two-for-one replacements, and the 3,000- to 3,600-horsepower locomotives offered in the mid-1960s were double the output of the earlier machines.

This book covers the critical three decades of diesel production from the end of World War II (when railroads replaced steam) through the mid-1970s (when railroads replaced the first diesels). It features a variety of models from the five major builders and is intended as a showcase of diesel operations, featuring many different models at work on a number of different lines. While many locomotives are portrayed, the book is not intended as a comprehensive diesel identification guide, nor does it pose to offer a detailed production catalog or complete roster.

The first decades of American dieselization offered unprecedented variety of motive power, and this book features many of the most common models, along with some of the more unusual and obscure types. Photographs were carefully selected to include period images from the steam-to-diesel transition period, along with period views from the 1960s and 1970s, but also more recent images of vintage diesels at work. Among the lasting legacies of some vintage diesel power has been its exceptional durability and longevity. Today, there are operating locomotives that have worked for more than five decades. Yet, some types, notably early road diesels built by Baldwin, were notoriously unreliable and were withdrawn from service after only a few years. Most commercially unsuccessful diesels have been gone for decades. A few rare and unusual diesels have been preserved, but most others are only remembered in photographs.

Chapter 1

Alco

Alco

To better compete for orders with locomotive giant Baldwin Locomotive Works, a host of comparatively small locomotive manufacturers joined together in 1901 to form the American Locomotive Company, long known by the acronym of its initials, Alco. Largest and most significant of Alco's constituent companies was The Schenectady Locomotive Works of Schenectady, New York. In later years this developed as Alco's primary locomotive works in the United States and gradually supplanted the other works that had helped form Alco. To build locomotives for the prosperous Canadian market, Alco acquired the Locomotive and Machine Company of Montreal Limited and changed its name to Montreal Locomotive Works (MLW) in 1908. Both the Schenectady and Montreal facilities manufactured diesel-electrics.

Although primarily a steam builder in it first decades, during the mid-1920s Alco played an important role in the first commercially successful diesel-electric. In 1925, General Electric, Ingersoll-Rand, and Alco formed a diesel-electric construction consortium, wherein Alco supplied mechanical components (primarily the carbodies and running gear). After a few years, Alco left this partnership to develop its own line of diesel switchers. During the late 1920s, Alco acquired a majority share in engine-builder McIntosh & Seymour. Using the M&S engine, Alco introduced a standard end-cab switcher in the early 1930s, and for a few years it was the leader in domestic diesel sales. However, during the 1930s Alco's efforts were eclipsed by Electro-Motive Corporation (known as its Electro-Motive Division after 1940). To better compete with Electro-Motive, in 1940 Alco and GE entered a formal arrangement for the construction and sale of diesel-electric locomotives. By this time, Alco had made formative progress as a builder of road-service diesels.

At request of the War Production Board, Alco focused wartime production on steam designs and diesel switchers. During the crucial years after the war, Alco-GE maintained the number-two position in the domestic locomotive market and sold large numbers of diesels in several key categories.

Its high-speed model PA/PB passenger diesel emulated Electro-Motive's successful E-unit, while the FA/FB road freight diesel was Alco's version of Electro-Motive's groundbreaking F-unit. Significant in Alco's catalog were its road-switcher designs. In 1940, Alco had adapted its S model switcher into a hood unit designed for both switching and roadwork and capable of handling freight or passenger assignments both singly or in multiple. The RS-1 road-switcher set an important precedent soon emulated by the other major diesel builders. After the war, Alco introduced a more powerful road switcher, the model RS-2. In 1950, Alco replaced the RS-2 with its more reliable RS-3, which proved to be one of its bestselling diesels (Louis A. Marre's *Diesel Locomotives: The First 50 Years* lists 366 RS-2s and 1,265 RS-3s sold to U.S. lines). Additional locomotives were built by MLW, and similar types were built and licensed for export.

Although Alco's partnership with GE ended in 1953, it continued to use GE components. Significantly, of the three big steam manufacturers (including Baldwin and Lima), only Alco survived the steam-to-diesel transition. In the mid-1950s, it introduced a new line of diesels based on its recently perfected 251 engine. This line is typified by the RS-11, a rugged 1,800-horsepower four-motor road switcher. The new engine and other technological improvements enabled Alco to survive the first rounds of the "horsepower war" in the late 1950s and 1960s.

In 1963, Alco introduced its improved Century series, as part of its final effort to improve its North American locomotive business. The series featured a variety of refinements that also gave Alco diesels a cleaner exterior design, which many observers consider to be the finest of the era. Century models used an improved designation system logically describing powered axles and horsepower. Each new Alco model used the "C" (for Century) followed by a three-digit number: the first digit indicated powered axles, the second and third represented approximate horsepower.

By this time, Alco was the weakest of the three diesel builders, and despite its best efforts, it ultimately faltered in the high-horsepower market. In 1968, it built its last locomotives, and in early 1969 it exited the U.S. market. In Canada, MLW continued to build locomotives derived from Alco's designs for a few more years.

Previous pages:
Many of Alco's most loyal customers were railroads that operated in the builder's home state of New York. Lehigh Valley bought a variety of Alco diesels, including these RS-11s and C-628s as seen at Sayre, Pennsylvania, on May 31, 1973. Lehigh Valley was one of several bankrupt railroads melded into Conrail on April 1, 1976. *R. R. Richardson photo, Doug Eisele collection*

Switchers needed a short wheelbase to negotiate tight curvature in industrial areas. San Francisco Belt Railroad Alco S-2 No. 25 works street trackage along the Embarcadero on December 14, 1975. In its heyday, the railroad operated 75 miles of industrial and street trackage, largely around San Francisco's waterfront. As the city's industrial base declined, so did the railroad. The Belt no longer moves freight; today new tracks along the city's Embarcadero carry electric streetcars for the Municipal Railway. *Brian Jennison*

Massachusetts' Grafton & Upton Railroad is among the most unusual lines in the state. It began as a narrow gauge line, was later converted to standard gauge, then was electrified as an interurban, and today survives as a short-line freight carrier. In February 1963, a G&U Alco S-2 working cab-first moves freight at Grafton. *Jim Shaughnessy*

In the mid-1980s, Connecticut's K&L Feeds acquired former Central Vermont Railway Alco S-4 No. 8081. The freshly painted switcher reposes in the morning sun at CV's New London Yard on February 28, 1988. Today the locomotive is preserved at the Connecticut Eastern Railroad Museum in Willimantic. *Brian Solomon*

A view of the short hood on Genesee & Wyoming RS-1 No. 25 at Retsof, New York. This 1,000-horsepower Alco-GE road switcher was built for G&W in 1952. It was photographed 35 years later at Retsof, where it was still working for the same railroad. *Brian Solomon*

This detail shows the short hood and headlight on G&W RS-1 No. 1976. Built by Alco in May 1955 as G&W No. 30, the locomotive was renamed *E. P. McCloskey*, renumbered, and painted red, white, and blue for the American bicentennial. *Brian Solomon*

New York, Susquehanna & Western was among the earliest railroads to fully dieselize regular operations. By the end of World War II, it largely relied on Alco switchers and road switchers. On August 7, 1959, NYS&W RS-1 No. 231 was at Erie Railroad's Jersey City Terminal with a passenger train destined for Butler, New Jersey. *Richard Jay Solomon*

Rutland Railroad Alco RS-1 No. 405 was built by Alco-GE at Schenectady, New York, in November 1951. Less than two years later, GE dissolved its locomotive-building partnership with Alco, although it continued to supply Alco with primary electrical components. After its split with GE, Alco redesigned its locomotive line and introduced a new diesel prime mover. *Brian Solomon*

Green Mountain, now a component of the Vermont Rail System, is one of the last regular users of an Alco RS-1 road switcher and routinely assigns former Rutland Railroad No. 405 to passenger excursion service on old home rails. *Brian Solomon*

Green Mountain Railroad No. 405 leads an excursion on the old Rutland Railroad at Proctorville, Vermont, on October 9, 2004. Typically excursions operate between Bellows Falls and Chester, but on this day the route was extended beyond its normal limits to Proctorsville. Here the excursion met the daily freight from Rutland, Vermont, much to the excitement of local residents. *Brian Solomon*

Above: The versatility of the RS-1 allowed it to work a great variety of trains. Chicago & Western Indiana was one of Chicago's most obscure passenger carriers. In June 1961, C&WI Alco RS-1 No. 259 leads a short train near 16th Street. On the upper level a group of Rock Island Alco road switchers await duty for the evening suburban rush hour from LaSalle Street Station. *Richard Jay Solomon*

Opposite top: In January 1969, Vermont Railway RS-1s 404 and 402 lead a freight on the former Rutland Railroad between Emerald Lake and East Dorset, Vermont. Vermont Railway 404 was built for Duluth, South Shore & Atlantic in 1946 and acquired by Vermont Railway in 1967 to add to its fleet of former Rutland Railroad RS-1s. *Jim Shaughnessy*

Opposite bottom: The RS-1 was equally at home on the main line, out on a branch, or working in the yard. On August 19, 1972, Penn Central RS-1 No. 9910 was caught at the east end of Goodman Street Yard in Rochester, New York, on the famed former New York Central Water Level Route. Penn Central inherited RS-1s from all three of its constituent railroads. *R. R. Richardson photo, Doug Eisele collection*

New York Central painted RS-3 No. 8223 at Conrail's DeWitt Yard. Central had been one of Alco's best customers in steam days and continued to order large numbers of Alco products into the diesel era. While Central also placed substantial orders with Alco's competitors, it remained loyal to Alco right through the late 1960s. *Brian Solomon*

Left: This detail shows the short hood on New York Central No. 8223 wearing the classic lightning stripe livery. In their day, Central's legions of Alco road switchers were hardly worth a passing glance; today this preserved locomotive is viewed as a gem from the early days of dieselization. *Brian Solomon*

Below: New York Central No. 8223 as seen from the cab of an F-unit on the Adirondack Scenic Railroad at Thendera, New York, on July 22, 2004. Along with Electro-Motive's F-unit, the Alco RS-3 was among the most common locomotives built during the steam-to-diesel transition period. Adirondack Scenic Railroad uses a variety of vintage diesels to offer passenger excursions of former New York Central lines in upstate New York. *Brian Solomon*

On Providence & Worcester's first day of independent operation in 1973, a leased Delaware & Hudson RS-3 gleams in fresh P&W paint outside the Worcester engine house. Once a component of New Haven Railroad, P&W sought independence after New Haven's inclusion in the doomed Penn Central merger of the late 1960s. *Jim Shaughnessy*

Penn Central and Conrail repowered a number of RS-3s using EMD 567 engines salvaged from scrapped E-units. The repowered locomotives were designated RS-3M and operated in secondary service. On June 10, 1982, Conrail RS-3M No. 9905 leads the wire train on the old New Haven Railroad at Mount Vernon, New York. George W. Kowanski was the engineer that day and took the opportunity to make this rare photograph. *George W. Kowanski*

New Haven RS-3s rest in front of the Waterbury, Connecticut, railway station in June 1960. Today New Haven RS-3 No. 529 is preserved in operating condition on the Naugatuck Railroad, which operates through its namesake valley to the north of Waterbury. *Richard Jay Solomon*

Road switchers by nature were versatile machines suited to a variety of assignments. Rock Island was one of many railroads that assigned them to suburban service, where their rapid loading characteristics allowed them to maintain tight schedules. In July 1958, Rock Island No. 497 works a Chicago–Blue Island train. *Richard Jay Solomon*

Lehigh Valley Alco RS-3 No. 215 drills the yard at Manchester, New York, on October 17, 1971. Alcos were famous for their smoke shows when notched out rapidly; the 244 engine in particular was especially smoky. *R. R. Richardson photo, Doug Eisele collection*

Opposite bottom: Western Maryland had four RS-3s equipped with both dynamic brakes and steam generators, options which when combined mandated a high short hood. Only five RS-3s were built this way; the fifth went to the Pennsylvania Railroad and later was traded to the Lehigh Valley, becoming its No. 211. On May 13, 1972, a pair of WM FAs leads RS-3 No. 192 and an Electro-Motive F-unit at Hagerstown. In the 1950s, WM pioneered multiple-unit connections between Alco and Electro-Motive locomotives. *R. R. Richardson photo, Doug Eisele collection*

Freshly painted Battenkill Railroad RS-3 No. 605 is seen at Eagle Bridge, New York, on May 13, 1984. Formerly Vermont Railway No. 605, it has served Battenkill Railroad in the same paint livery for 25 years—longer than many other RS-3s worked American rails. *Jim Shaughnessy*

On October 20, 2009, Battenkill Railroad RS-3 No. 605 has just passed Shushan, New York, on its run to Eagle Bridge, where the railroad interchanges freight with CP Rail and Pan Am Southern's Boston & Maine route. The Battenkill operates a few miles of former Delaware & Hudson secondary lines in eastern New York State. *Brian Solomon*

A detail of the short hood on No. 605 shows the classic Hancock air whistle and twin sealed-beam headlight. In 2010, this was among the last as-built RS-3s in revenue freight service in North America. More than 1,750 RS-2s and RS-3s were built, but today only a handful survives outside of museums. *Brian Solomon*

A quartet of Alco FA/FBs leading an eastward freight on the Boston & Albany approaches the west portal of State Line Tunnel near Canaan, New York. New York Central operated the largest fleet of Alco FA/FB cab units. *Jim Shaughnessy*

New York Central's Alco FA-2 freight diesels rest between assignments at the former West Shore yards in North Bergen, New Jersey, on April 13, 1958. Alco's FA/FB was a carbody type that emulated Electro-Motive's successful F-unit. Central routinely operated FA/FBs in multiple for more than two decades, although in later years it was common to find them mixed with other models. *Richard Jay Solomon*

In the late 1940s, a nearly new A-B-A set of Alco FA diesels exits the east portal of State Line Tunnel with an eastward freight. In 1947, Alco diesels began supplanting Boston & Albany's famous Lima-built Berkshire-type steam locomotives on road freights. By 1951, the road was fully dieselized, making it the first major component of the New York Central system to be operated entirely with diesels. *Robert A. Buck*

Erie Lackawanna FA-1 No. 7254 catches the sun east of Buffalo at Bison Yard in Sloan, New York, in July 1968. EL inherited its FA/FBs from the Erie Railroad. Powered by Alco's 244 engine, the FA-1 was rated at 1,500 horsepower. While many railroads used FA models into the 1960s, these Alco road units were not as well regarded as the EMD F-units and had become rare by 1970. *Doug Eisele collection*

An A-B-A set of Baltimore & Ohio Alco FAs wearing the as-delivered two-tone blue leads a westward freight at Creston in east-central Ohio in the mid-1950s. B&O operated a moderate-sized fleet of Alco FA/FB-2s built between 1950 and 1953. Rated at 1,600 horsepower, these were nominally more powerful than Electro-Motive's F7, which was a more common type on B&O lines in the 1950s. *J. William Vigrass*

In the early 1960s, just a few years after the fateful merger between Erie Railroad and one-time competitor Delaware, Lackawanna & Western, Erie-Lackawanna FA-1 No. 7321 rolls across a weed-grown diamond crossing near Campbell Hall, New York. Erie Railroad connected with the New Haven at nearby Maybrook, New York, not far from Campbell Hall. This served as gateway to New England, which resulted in considerable freight interchange between the two lines. *Richard Jay Solomon*

A Southern Pacific Alco PA cab leads the *Shasta Daylight* at Dunsmuir, California, in 1961. The Alco PA employed a single turbocharged 244 engine, which was four-cycle diesel introduced in 1944 to generate 2,000 horsepower. The later PA-2/PB-2s were even more powerful and rated at 2,250 horsepower. Greater output, more rugged traction motors, and dynamic braking were among the reasons that SP favored the PA for passenger services on heavily graded routes.
Bob Morris

An Alco PA and EMD F7A work upgrade in the Colorado Front Range with Rio Grande's *Yampa Valley Mail* in 1963. Although PAs and Fs would have rarely worked together on most railroads, such combinations were not uncommon on the Rio Grande. *Jim Shaughnessy*

In 1961, Santa Fe Railway PA No. 75 leads the eastward *San Francisco Chief* across the Western Pacific crossing at Stockton, California. Santa Fe was among the last original buyers to operate PAs in passenger service. In the late 1960s, Delaware & Hudson acquired four Santa Fe PAs, and today two of these are preserved. *Bob Morris*

Just after 11:00 a.m. on July 16, 1958, warbonnet-painted Alco PAs lead Santa Fe train No. 13 west from Chicago's Dearborn Station. The first Alco PA was symbolically assigned Alco's 75,000 builder number and after tests on Lehigh Valley was sold to Santa Fe, becoming its No. 51.
Richard Jay Solomon

In 1961, a year after the Erie-Lackawanna merger, an Alco PA in full Erie paint idles at Lackawanna's Hoboken Terminal on the Jersey side of the Hudson opposite Manhattan. On the left is a set of Lackawanna F3s, and looming through the smog is the famous Empire State Building. Among the consolidations facilitated by the merger was Erie abandoning its Jersey City terminal in favor of Lackawanna's Hoboken Terminal. *Richard Jay Solomon*

On May 10, 1959, Lehigh Valley Alco PA diesels are exchanged for a Pennsylvania Railroad GG1 electric near Newark, New Jersey. Lehigh Valley passenger trains served Pennsy's Penn Station in New York City, which required the change of locomotives because diesels are not allowed in the tunnels beneath the Hudson River. Once famous for its *Black Diamond*, Lehigh Valley ended all passenger service in 1961. *Richard Jay Solomon*

Three of D&H's former Santa Fe Alco PAs are seen inside Colonie Shops in October 1973. D&H was the last railroad in the United States to operate classic PA diesels. D&H sent its PAs to Morrison-Knudsen for rebuilding in the late 1970s and then leased them to Boston's Massachusetts Bay Transportation Authority for a stint in suburban service before selling them to a New Jersey–based leasing company that shipped them to Mexico. *Jim Shaughnessy*

D&H bought secondhand PA diesels for passenger service. However, after the advent of Amtrak in 1971 temporarily left D&H without a passenger train, it assigned PAs to freight work. Later, when passenger services were restored between Albany and Montreal, the PAs were rebuilt and put back to work as intended. This rare photograph shows all four PAs on D&H's southward SC-1 local freight running along the shore of Lake Champlain at Port Henry, New York. *Jim Shaughnessy*

Three Delaware & Hudson PAs lead the southward *Susquehanna Valley Special* excursion on the Albany main south of Albany, New York, on September 29, 1973. Although D&H was one of the best known operators of PAs, the railroad was one of the few operators that had not bought them new from Alco. *Brian Jennison*

New York, Chicago & St. Louis Railroad was a mouthful, so the line was better known as the Nickel Plate Road—abbreviated as NKP. A pair of NKP PA diesels arrives at Buffalo with an eastward passenger train. Nickel Plate's were among the most attractively painted Alco passenger locomotives. Built by Alco-GE in 1947 and 1948, Nickel Plate Road's PAs were all rated at 2,000 horsepower. *Jay Williams collection*

In 1947, Pennsylvania Railroad bought 10 PAs and 5 cab-less PB "boosters" from Alco. These had been intended for passenger service, but within a decade the Pennsy reassigned them to less glamorous jobs. On May 4, 1957, Nos. 5751A and 5757A work as helpers along with a venerable I1s Decapod on freight climbing northward on the Elmira Branch. *Jim Shaughnessy*

In March 1958, NKP Alco PA No. 183 leads No. 7 westbound at Cleggville, Cleveland, Ohio. In 1962, NKP traded its PA fleet back to Alco on an order for RS-36 road switchers. *W. McCaleb photo, Jay Williams collection*

Falls Road Railroad Alco RS-11 No. 1802 is a former Nickel Plate Road locomotive and one of several RS-11s operated by parent company Genesee Valley Transportation. The RS-11 is powered by a 1,800-horsepower 251 diesel engine. *Brian Solomon*

On July 17, 2006, Falls Road Railroad Alco RS-11 No. 1802 works its way east with a local freight on the former New York Central Falls Road from Lockport to Brockport. Back in New York Central times this was Alco territory, and today it is again. *Brian Solomon*

New York Central's Falls Road provided a direct route from Rochester to Niagara Falls, New York, and served through freight and passenger trains. Today it is just a dead-end branch used for local freight traffic. *Brian Solomon*

In July 1963, a new New York Central RS-32 leads an eastward freight down the Hudson Division toward New York City. Central bought the 2,000-horsepower RS-32 for use in fast freight service. This was a relatively unusual type; the only other railroad to buy the model new was Southern Pacific. *Richard Jay Solomon*

Today, Genesee Valley Transportation's Falls Road Railroad short line routinely assigns former New York Central RS-32 No. 2035 to local work on the old New York Central Falls Road route. On October 13, 2008, engineer Russ Young switches sidings serving a new ethanol plant on the line. *Brian Solomon*

A close-up shows the Genesee Valley Transportation nose decal on Falls Road Railroad No. 2035, working its namesake branch. Among the characteristics of the classic vintage RS-32 is the long one-piece front windshield that spans the width of the nose section. All RS-32s were built with low short hoods to give the crew better forward visibility. *Brian Solomon*

Lehigh Valley C-420 No. 415 is seen in Cornell Red at Sayre, Pennsylvania, on March 14, 1976. In less than a month, Lehigh Valley would be absorbed by Conrail, and this C-420 would be one of 12 conveyed to Delaware & Hudson. D&H was expanded as a part of the federally sponsored creation of Conrail in order to provide the guise of rail competition over selected Conrail routes. *Bill Dechau photo, Doug Eisele collection*

Lehigh Valley C-420 No. 406 works an eastward freight through Odessa, New York. The C-420 was built in both low short hood and high hood variations. Lehigh Valley, Lehigh & Hudson River, Monon, Long Island, and Louisville & Nashville were among the railroads to order this attractively designed road switcher. *R. R. Richardson photo, Doug Eisele collection*

On October 5, 1974, Lehigh Valley No. 415 and two other LV C-420s lead an eastward freight. All are in Lehigh's as-delivered gray and yellow livery. With the introduction of the Century series in 1963, the C-420 was the 2,000-horsepower model that succeeded the short-lived RS-32. Where only 35 RS-32s were built, the C-420 accounted for 131 units, including a pair sold to Mexico. *R. R. Richardson photo, Doug Eisele collection*

Left and below: Maine Eastern runs trains on the former Maine Central Rockland Branch east from Brunswick to its namesake. Among its freight operations is the short haul from Dragon Cement in Thomaston to shipping barges at Rockland. In August 2004, New Jersey's Morristown & Erie—operator of Maine Eastern—provided power for the cement train in the form of a former CP Rail C-424. The three-car train of pressurized cement hoppers is seen on its way through Rockland on the way to the docks. *Both photos Brian Solomon*

Opposite: CP Rail C-424 No. 4206 catches the sun at Guelph Junction, Ontario, on September 24, 1988. This Montreal-built locomotive was very similar to its Schenectady-built counterparts. Alco's longtime Canadian affiliate Montreal Locomotive Works not only built Alco-designed locomotives for the Canadian market, but it continued to build locomotives for several years after Alco ended domestic production in 1969. *Brian Solomon*

Genesee Valley Transportation's Delaware-Lackawanna operates a network of former Delaware, Lackawanna & Western and Delaware & Hudson lines radiating from Scranton, Pennsylvania. In September 1996, D-L C-425 No. 2452 works the old D&H main line south of downtown Scranton. One of several former Erie-Lackawanna Alcos operated by D-L, No. 2452 wears a livery similar to that of the old E-L. *Brian Solomon*

Above: Former Erie-Lackawanna C-425 No. 2461 leads Delaware-Lackawanna's PT98 working west toward Scranton on the former DL&W main line on its return trip from Slateford Junction. In its heyday, this was a busy triple-track main line serving as a corridor for coal and manifest freight as well as express passenger trains. *Brian Solomon*

Left: In the 1960s, Erie-Lackawanna urged Alco to boost output of its C-424 to 2,500 horsepower to match General Electric's U25B. E-L ordered a dozen of the new C-425s. Today, short-line operator Genesee Valley Transportation operates several former E-L C-425s on its lines in New York and Pennsylvania. Old E-L No. 2461 catches the morning sun at Scranton just a short distance from the old Delaware, Lackawanna & Western shops. *Brian Solomon*

A short portion of the old Delaware, Lackawanna & Western main line in western New York State is run by Bath & Hammondport. On May 9, 2007, a pair of C-424Ms lead B&H's freight toward Painted Post, New York, on the line that once hosted famous named passenger trains, such as the *Lackawanna Limited* and the streamlined *Phoebe Snow*. *Brian Solomon*

B&H C-424M No. 422 leads a freight working the former DL&W main line near Savona, New York, on May 9, 2007. Among the perceived advantages of the Erie-Lackawanna merger was the ability to consolidate redundant facilities and parallel routes. Erie-Lackawanna favored former Erie Railroad routes west of Binghamton; as a result much of the old DL&W was downgraded. This segment of old DL&W main line now serves as a short-line branch, where as late as 1964 it carried through freight and passenger trains to Buffalo. *Brian Solomon*

Built by Alco in 1963 as Erie-Lackawanna No. 2414, B&H C-424M No. 422 has had a long history. In the 1970s, it was acquired by Delaware & Hudson (No. 451), which had the locomotive rebuilt as a C-424M, lowering output from 2,400 to 2,000 horsepower. Today, it is back on old home rails working for B&H, one of several short lines affiliated with Livonia, Avon & Lakeville that operate segments of former E-L trackage. *Brian Solomon*

A cab detail of Western New York & Pennsylvania No. 430 shows the distinctive angled windshield, contoured cab roof, and classification lights that are unique to Alco's Century series. Introduced in 1967 to compete with Electro-Motive's GP40, the 3,000-horsepower C-430 was the most powerful of Alco's four-motor Centuries. No. 430 was originally New York Central No. 2050 and later served Penn Central, Conrail, and New York, Susquehanna & Western. *Brian Solomon*

On July 19, 2009, WNY&P No. 430 leads two other Centuries with the westward HNME (Hornell, New York, to Meadville, Pennsylvania) near Andover, New York, on the former Erie Railroad main line. In the early 1990s, Conrail discontinued operations on the former Erie west of Hornell, yet a decade later the line was revived and reopened by WNY&P. *Brian Solomon*

WNY&P is a short line affiliated with Livonia, Avon & Lakeville that operates on portions of the old Erie Railroad and Pennsylvania Railroad using an eclectic fleet of Alco and Montreal Locomotive Works diesels. WNY&P Alco C-430 No. 430 is seen at Allegany Yard, in Olean, New York, on October 11, 2008. *Brian Solomon*

Lehigh Valley Alco C-628s lead a westward freight under the Hamilton Street bridge in Allentown, Pennsylvania, in February 1975. After Lehigh Valley was melded into the federally planned Conrail system in 1976, its six-motor Alcos were reassigned to other routes. Most finished up their service in the late 1970s working mineral trains on the former Pennsylvania Railroad out of Mingo Junction, Ohio. *George W. Kowanski*

In late winter sun in early March 1973 at Crescent, New York, a quartet of Lehigh Valley Alco C-628s work eastward on a Delaware & Hudson/Lehigh Valley pool freight destined for Mechanicville, New York. Lehigh Valley ultimately acquired 17 C-628s, including 9 former Monon units. *Jim Shaughnessy*

Lehigh Valley C-628 No. 636 rests with another Century on the ready tracks near the railroad's steam-era shop complex at Sayre, Pennsylvania, on May 24, 1972. No. 636 was former Monon No. 404, one of nine units the Midwestern line traded back to Alco after just a few years in service. *R. R. Richardson photo, Doug Eisele collection*

In May 1965, three new Alco C-628s deliver 8,250 horsepower on a southward Delaware & Hudson freight reaching the crest of Richmondville Hill. For a very short time, Alco's 2,750-horsepower C-628 was the most powerful single-engine single-unit diesel-electric on the commercial market in North America. More powerful "double diesels" were bought by Union Pacific and Southern Pacific using pairs of prime movers. *Jim Shaughnessy*

Monon bought nine Alco C-628s, which it intended to use in unit coal train service. When the coal contract fizzled, the railroad operated the units in regular freight service before trading them back to Alco on an order for less powerful but more versatile C-420s. Monon No. 408 was photographed at Bloomington, Indiana, in November 1965. *Jay Williams collection*

In May 1968, new Alco C-628s sit outside Alco's Schenectady Works awaiting shipment to Nacionales de Mexico. In less than a year, Alco would cease locomotive production, ending a long history of continuous locomotive construction at this site. N. de M. bought 32 C-628s from Alco and was one of three railroads to work these locomotives south of the border. *Jim Shaughnessy*

On July 24, 1997, Cape Breton & Central Nova Scotia freight No. 305 works westward with M-630 No. 2034 climbing the 1.5 percent grade to Marshy Hope, Nova Scotia. CB&CNS operated 245 miles of trackage spun off from Canadian National Railways in 1993. Initially the railroad used a mix of secondhand Alco-designed diesels built by affiliate Montreal Locomotive Works to move its freight trains. *Brian Solomon*

Cape Breton & Central Nova Scotia M-630 catches the setting sun at Afton, Nova Scotia, on July 25, 1997. CB&CNS continued to operate six-motor MLWs in road service in Canada for a few years after Canadian National and CP Rail had disposed of their big Century fleets. *Brian Solomon*

Cape Breton & Central Nova Scotia's insignia on the side of an M-630. Although Alco ended locomotive production at its Schenectady, New York, plant, MLW continued to build diesels to Alco designs for a few more years. *Brian Solomon*

On the evening of July 25, 1997, a trio of Cape Breton & Central Nova Scotia M-630s labor on the climb to Marshy Hope. Alcos were known for their great pulling power at slow speeds, but on this day the grade got the better of the locomotives and the crew needed to "double the hill" (take the tonnage up in two trips). *Brian Solomon*

By the mid-1990s, six-motor Alco locomotives were an anachronism, thus giving the remote CB&CNS an antique mystique. M-630 No. 2034, named *Sir Conan Doyle,* leads westward freight 305. *Brian Solomon*

Just after noontime on July 26, 1997, CB&CNS M-630 No. 2003 rolls past the general store in Merigomish, Nova Scotia. The days of the six-motor Alco working heavy freight on CB&CNS were short-lived; after a few years the railroad replaced them with less colorful diesels. *Brian Solomon*

The isolated 260-mile Cartier Railway between Port Cartier and Mont Wright was built in the 1950s to tap enormous iron ore reserves in northeastern Quebec. Three M-636s/C-636s with an empty ore train growl upgrade through wilderness in the Sept-Îles National Park many miles north of Port Cartier. *Brian Solomon*

Loaded ore trains on the Cartier are not allowed great speed, yet this panned shot of Cartier No. 82 from July 12, 1997, makes it appear as if the big Century is really moving. An order for six-motor General Electric diesels in 2001 ended Alco/MLW supremacy on this isolated line. *Brian Solomon*

Three C-636/M-636s led by Cartier No. 82 bring a heavy ore train south of Dog siding in Quebec's Sept-Îles National Park. The remoteness and wonderful scenery of this line are great attractions for photographers. *Brian Solomon*

Western New York & Pennsylvania has acquired several former Cartier six-motor Alco/MLW diesels for work on its lines radiating out of Olean, New York. On October 12, 2008, WNY&P No. 637 works the westward HNME (Hornell, New York, to Meadville, Pennsylvania) on the old Erie Railroad main line near Cambridge Springs, Pennsylvania. *Brian Solomon*

In the 1960s, Erie-Lackawanna routinely dispatched Alco Centuries on long freight trains making their way to Midwestern gateways. Four decades later, old Alco diesels ply the line with local freight. On October 8, 2009, the sounds of Alco 251 engines permeate the morning mist as WNY&P's HNME works west of Union City, Pennsylvania, with M-636 No. 637 in the lead. *Brian Solomon*

WNY&P M-636 No. 637 rolls through Saegertown on the last lap of its run from Hornell, New York, to Meadville, Pennsylvania, over the former Erie Railroad main line. *Brian Solomon*

Chapter 2
Baldwin

Baldwin

ounded by Matthias W. Baldwin, the Baldwin Locomotive Works began building steam locomotives in 1831 and at the dawn of the diesel age was America's oldest surviving locomotive manufacturer. Although it was a master of steam locomotive construction and early to anticipate the practicality of the diesel, Baldwin delayed in developing commercial diesel-electric technology. However, in 1931, Baldwin acquired established engine manufacturers I. P. Morris and De La Vergne and transferred production to its Eddystone, Pennsylvania, plant with the aim of developing a diesel locomotive engine. Eddystone was a relatively modern plant, having been completed in the 1920s as a spacious replacement for Baldwin's old facilities in downtown Philadelphia. Initially, Baldwin constructed its diesels in the steam locomotive tender shop, because the diesel bodies were similar in construction to tenders.

Baldwin's first commercial diesels, and by far its greatest success in the diesel market, were switchers it introduced in the late 1930s and improved after World War II. It built approximately 1,900 diesel

switchers during its two decades in the diesel business, offering models in the 660- to 800- and 1,000- to 1,200-horsepower range. Of these, the 1,000-horsepower types were the most common.

During the war, Baldwin's efforts to develop high-horsepower road diesels were unsuccessful; after the war, it continued to build some respectable road switchers, but its postwar approach to road diesels yielded eclectic and curious designs that compared poorly with those of its competition. Most lasted only a few years in service before requiring rebuilding, often with Electro-Motive engines.

In 1950, Baldwin merged with Lima-Hamilton. Lima had been the smallest of the "big three" commercial steam locomotive manufacturers. It was only in the diesel business for about two years following the acquisition. Although the company retained the Lima name and was known afterward as Baldwin-Lima-Hamilton, it discontinued Lima's diesel line in favor of the more successful Baldwin diesels. Despite improvements to its locomotives, Baldwin found it increasingly difficult to compete and exited commercial locomotive manufacturing in 1956. Its switchers proved the longest lived; as late as 2010, a few survive in freight service on North American short lines. Although bought by a variety of railroads, Baldwin's road locomotives were few in number compared with the vast quantities of Alco and Electro-Motive products used to dieselize the railroads following World War II.

Compared with Alco and Electro-Motive, Baldwin's total diesel production was relatively small, yet between 1937 and 1956 it constructed roughly three dozen different diesel models for domestic applications. Baldwin's variety, combined with its relative obscurity, has long made its diesels fascinating to locomotive enthusiasts. Many Baldwin models were unique to specific railroads. For example, Pennsylvania Railroad was the only line to buy the DR-6-4-2000 with the "shark-nose" body style. Other lines bought similar DR-6-4-2000s that featured the "baby-face" body style. With Baldwin, however, looks can be deceiving, as different body styles were used on models with nearly identical specifications. Furthermore, in some situations, entirely different models had similar body styles. For example, no less than three domestic models were built using the shark-nose body, yet one of these models, the DR-4-4-15, was also built with the baby-face design.

Baldwin used a different system for operating locomotives in multiple than other builders. For this reason, Baldwin diesels tended not to work with other builders' diesels. Some railroads, such as New York Central, later rebuilt Baldwins, increasing their operating life and making them more versatile.

Baldwin's diesels had a distinctive sound to them as well. The De La Vergne diesel was a four-cycle design that Baldwin built in various configurations using both normally aspirated and turbocharged designs. It had maximum rotational speed of 625 rpm (much slower than the engines of other builders) and made a ponderous sound at lower throttle positions while producing a thrashing at full throttle.

Baldwin was a pioneer of the six-motor diesel-electric, which were among the company's best diesel products. These were designed for high-tractive effort applications and known for their ability to haul heavy tonnage at slow speeds for extended periods. A few railroads bought Baldwins for passenger service, but these locomotives tended to fair poorly and were typically reassigned to freight work after just a few years. As a result, photographs of Baldwin diesels hauling passenger trains are relatively rare.

Oakland Terminal Baldwin DS-4-4-1000 No. 101 works yard trackage off Wood Street in Oakland, California, on November 4, 1980. OT bought the locomotive new in 1948. Now owned by the Pacific Locomotive Association and stored in Niles Canyon at Brightside, California, it is one of several preserved Baldwin diesels in the United States. *Brian Jennison*

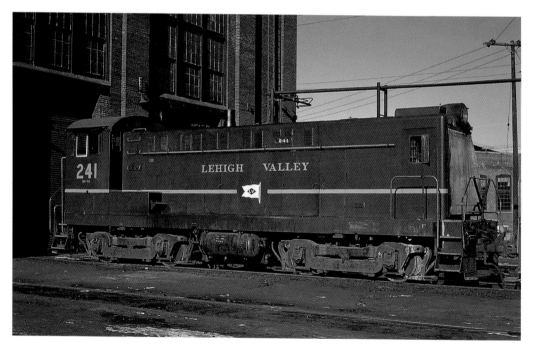

Many railroads got their first taste for Baldwin switchers during World War II, when Baldwin was limited to the production of diesel switchers and steam locomotives. Lehigh Valley bought five VO1000-type switchers in 1944. Nearly 30 years later, on February 13, 1973, LV No. 241—a Baldwin-Lima-Hamilton S-12 from 1950—rests at the company shops in Sayre, Pennsylvania. *Doug Eisele*

Sierra Railroad S-12 No. 44 works east of Oakdale, California, at Cooperstown on April 3, 1993. Although Sierra bought some of its Baldwin diesels new, this locomotive came secondhand from Sharon Steel. Sierra is one of a few railroads that continue to operate Baldwins in freight service decades after Baldwin exited the business. *Brian Solomon*

California Western DS-4-4-1000 switcher No. 53 was built new for the U.S. government in July 1949. Many California short lines acquired Baldwin diesels in the 1940s and 1950s and continued to operate them decades after Baldwin ended locomotive production and after larger railroads replaced Baldwins with EMD products. *Brian Jennison*

California Western RS-12 No. 56 leads Stillwell passenger cars on an excursion between Willits and Fort Bragg on July 1, 1976. The railroad's gas cars are known as "Skunk Trains"; when these prove inadequate to handle passenger loads, locomotive-hauled Super Skunks take over. *Brian Jennison*

California Western RS-12 No. 56 leads a "Super Skunk" excursion between Willits and Fort Bragg on July 13, 1985. Baldwin's RS-12 was a 1,200-horsepower road switcher designed for light road work and was well suited to short-line and branch-line operation. *Brian Jennison*

Although standard today, in the 1950s six-motor diesels were an operational anomaly. On July 28, 1958, a pair of Chesapeake & Ohio's Baldwin-built AS-616s grinds past the tower at Covington, Kentucky, with a long cut of coal hoppers. The AS-616 was among Baldwin's more successful efforts and was generally well regarded for heavy slow-speed work. The AS-616 was the successor to Baldwin's DRS-6-6-1500 and was nominally more powerful (rated at 1,600 horsepower to the older model's 1,500 horsepower). *Richard Jay Solomon*

Baldwin's heavy road switcher was powered with the 608SC engine and was initially rated at 1,500 horsepower. It was offered to railroads as a four-motor with either B-B or A1A trucks, or as a six-motor with C-C trucks. These types were respectively designated as models DRS-4-4-1500, DRS-6-4-1500, and DRS-6-6-1500. Erie-Lackawanna DRS-6-6-1500 No. 1156 was photographed at Buffalo, New York, on October 4, 1970. *Doug Eisele*

Ore-hauling Bessemer & Lake Erie operated an eclectic fleet of six-motor diesels a generation before six-motor types were standard power on other freight-hauling lines. B&LE's DRS-6-6-1500 No. 403 works at Albion, Pennsylvania, on June 7, 1970. It emerged from Baldwin's Eddystone plant 20 years earlier and enjoyed a relatively long career hauling heavy tonnage. *Doug Eisele*

In 1974, D&H acquired the last active pair of shark-nose diesels from a Pennsylvania-based scrap dealer. Originally New York Central locomotives, these had been among nine RF-16s that worked on the Pennsylvania mineral-hauling Monongahela Railway. They are pictured at Mechanicville shortly after their arrival on D&H property. *Jim Shaughnessy*

Delaware & Hudson RF-16 No. 1216 is shown at Mechanicville, New York, on February 15, 1975. By the time D&H acquired these "sharks," the type was all but extinct elsewhere. D&H operated them for just a few years before selling them to a short line. Although they have not operated in many years, both surviving sharks remain extant. *Jim Shaughnessy*

Baldwin's RF-16s were designed and geared for freight service, making passenger excursions such as this one a rare occurrence. On September 20, 1975, D&H's famous pair of former New York Central RF-16s leads an excursion destined for Whitehall and the rarely traveled Washington Branch. *Jim Shaughnessy*

Pennsylvania Railroad RF-16 No. 9595 rests at Cleveland's Kinsman Yard on July 11, 1958. The Pennsy, like many owners of Baldwin road diesels, tended to assign them to very heavy freights; Pennsy, New York Central, and Baltimore & Ohio all operated shark-nose models in mineral service. Today it seems strange that streamlined diesels would have spent so much time working away from the public eye in obscure freight service. *Richard Jay Solomon*

In May 1963 Central Railroad of New Jersey baby-face DR 4-4-1500s growl across a highway overpass with freight in tow. CNJ's Baldwin road diesels were among the longest to survive in service under their original ownership without repowering. *Richard Jay Solomon*

New York Central was one of three railroads to order Baldwin's four-motor road-freight diesel model DR 4-4-1500 in the baby-face body style. Although they looked substantially different, the early freight-service shark-nose units—those on B trucks rated at 1,500 horsepower—carried the same model designation as their baby-face counterparts. Later sharks were rated at 1,600 horsepower, designated model RF-16. On June 21, 1953, an A-B-A set of DR 4-4-1500s works Central's Selkirk hump yard. *Jim Shaughnessy*

Above: New York Central bought two A-B-A sets of Baldwin's DR-6-4-1500 baby-face streamlined passenger diesels. The only other taker was Seaboard Air Line. Central's were poorly regarded. Originally they rode on Commonwealth trucks and were known as "Gravel Gerties" because of their rough ride. Later the trucks were replaced, as was Baldwin's prime mover. Seen here in Collinwood after repowering with EMD's reliable 567 engine, Baldwin No. 3606 is paired with a similarly repowered Fairbanks-Morse "Erie-built." *J. William Vigrass*

Opposite top: Pennsy's big sharks—the 2,000-horsepower units carried on A1A trucks, designated as class BP20s by the railroad and model DR-6-4-2000 by the builder—were built in 1948 for long-distance passenger service but were bumped within a decade to lesser duties. In June 1964, BP20 No. 5773 hits a grade crossing on the New York & Long Branch as the rain lashes down. Slow film mandated creative photographic technique, so Richard Jay Solomon used his Leica range finder to pan the distinctive Baldwin profile. *Richard Jay Solomon*

Opposite bottom: Between assignments in suburban service on New Jersey's New York & Long Branch route, Pennsylvania Railroad DR-6-4-2000 No. 5770 rests at a diesel shop in the New Jersey Meadows on May 10, 1959. This date was the ninetieth anniversary of the famous "golden spike," when Central Pacific and Union Pacific met at Promontory, Utah—not that this mattered one iota to Pennsy or the lowly shark! *Richard Jay Solomon*

Chapter 3
Electro-Motive

Electro-Motive

GeneRal Motors' Electro-Motive Division—commonly known by the initials EMD after 1940—was the largest producer of diesel-electrics in the three decades following World War II. Its products effectively defined the diesel-electric as a road locomotive, and its innovations proved to American railroads that diesels could match the performance of steam while substantially lowering operating costs.

In 1930, General Motors acquired internal combustion engine manufacturer Winton Engine Company, along with gas-electric railcar designer Electro-Motive Company. During the next few years, these new GM subsidiaries refined diesel-electric locomotive technology and established the lightweight streamlined diesel-power car. The company rapidly adapted this technology for use as a standalone locomotive. As its technology and business matured, Electro-Motive developed diesel-electric switchers, then high-speed passenger and heavy freight locomotives, and finally road switchers.

Keys to GM's success included compact, high-output, two-cycle engine designs; a carefully thought-out design process that ensured maximum component reliability and compatibility; automotive-like production processes that minimized per-unit costs and kept engineering differences between models to a minimum; successful marketing; attractive locomotives; and attentive customer service.

Electro-Motive's first diesel efforts were custom-designed power cars for lightweight, articulated streamlined passenger trains. Yet, at the time, switchers were the largest commercial diesel-electric market, and in 1936, Electro-Motive began production of standard end-cab diesel switchers.

In 1937, Electro-Motive introduced its streamlined E-units for fast road passenger service. The E-unit's truss-supported carbody was integral to the structure of the locomotive and was universally adopted as the standard for diesel road units of the early steam-to-diesel transition period. Initially powered by a pair of Winton diesels, the early E-units were rated at 1,800 horsepower per unit and typically operated with one cab-equipped "A" unit leading one or two cab-less "B" units. All E-units rode on a pair of A1A six-wheel trucks (outside axles powered and center axle unpowered) designed by Martin Blomberg, who employed a system of outside swing hangers using both elliptical and helical springs to provide great stability at speed.

In 1938, Electro-Motive introduced the more reliable 567 diesel engine in place of Winton 201A diesel, and pairs of 12-cylinder, 1,000-horsepower 567s were used in the E3 through E6 models. EMD introduced the much-improved E7 in 1945, and it soon proved the bestselling passenger locomotive of the postwar period. Always looking to improve its line, EMD succeeded its E7 with the 2,250-horsepower E8 in 1949. In turn, this model was succeeded by the 2,400-horsepower E9 in 1955. Although the most powerful of E-units, with the longest production run of any E model, the E9 had lower production totals than either the E7 or E8 due to the sharp decline in intercity passenger services.

The FT model freight diesel was Electro-Motive's most influential locomotive. Quietly introduced in 1939, it soon demonstrated Electro-Motive's exceptional diesel-electric capabilities in heavy road-freight service and set the standard for road diesels for the next a decade. Like the E-unit, the FT used a carbody design, but each unit was powered by a single 16-cylinder 567 engine and rode on four-wheel Blomberg-designed trucks.

In its original configuration, the FT was designed to operate as an A-B-B-A four-unit set rated at 5,400 horsepower. The FT remained in production through 1945, when it was succeeded by the more powerful and more reliable F3 model. Where the individual FT unit was rated at 1,350 horsepower, each F3 was rated at 1,500 horsepower. In 1949, the F3 was succeeded by the even more reliable F7, a model that proved one of Electro-Motive's most popular postwar types. This was supplanted in 1954 by the 1,750-horsepower F9. Although the F-unit was originally aimed at the freight market, EMD introduced several variations designed for passenger work: FP7/FP9s featured larger steam generators necessary for passenger-car heating, while the FL9 was a dual-mode type ordered exclusively by the New Haven Railroad for service in New York City third-rail territory.

EMD did not make a serious effort to compete for road-switcher sales until it introduced the four-motor "general purpose" GP7 in 1949. The GP7's exceptional versatility rapidly displaced orders for the more specialized models in the early 1950s. In 1954, EMD introduced the GP9, an improved road switcher rated at 1,750 horsepower that proved significantly more reliable than earlier designs. This became one of the company's most popular locomotives; some still work short lines in 2010. Electro-Motive also offered six-

Previous pages:
Electro-Motive's F-unit is one of the twentieth century's most iconic locomotives. Thousands of these locomotives hauled trains all across North America. In 2009, Wabash F7A No. 1189 and Norfolk Southern's executive Fs pose for photographers at the Monticello Railway Museum at Monticello, Illinois. *Chris Guss*

Metra F40C No. 614 approaches Chicago's A2 Tower in June 2004 where former Milwaukee Road lines cross those of the former Chicago & North Western. Externally, F40Cs had more in common with the F45 than with the F40PH design of the mid-1970s. A pair of Metra F40PH-2s can be seen on the tracks beyond. *Brian Solomon.*

On August 21, 1994, Wisconsin & Southern GP9 No. 4491, facing long hood first, rests at the west end of the former Milwaukee Road line to Prairie du Chien, Wisconsin. This old Electro-Motive locomotive began life as a Rock Island GP18 but was later heavily rebuilt as a GP9. *Brian Solomon*

Gulf, Mobile & Ohio's *Alton Limited* departs St. Louis for Chicago led by a pair of EMD E7s on July 22, 1958. The E7 was EMD's most popular passenger locomotive. *Richard Jay Solomon*

motor road switchers, initially with its "special duty" SD7, later followed by the SD9, and then more powerful models.

By the late 1950s, EMD was focusing production on more powerful road switchers. It introduced the 2,000-horsepower GP20 in 1961, followed by the 2,250-horsepower GP30 in 1962, and the 2,500-horsepower GP35/SD35 in 1963. Electro-Motive's introduction of the more powerful and more reliable 645 series engine in the mid-1960s resulted in the 3,000-horsepower

GP40/SD40 and the 3,600-horsepower SD45. The high-horsepower units achieved greater power through application of a turbocharger; however, EMD also offered the 2,000-horsepower GP38/SD38 with a normally aspirated engine. These 645-engine diesels set new standards for reliability. In the 1970s, the six-motor SD40/SD40-2 emerged as the preferred North American locomotive. Thousands of this model were ordered, and it brought an end to many of the older and more specialized locomotives featured in these pages.

Above: Electro-Motive diesels were by far the most common of the postwar period. Working in Chicago on March 22, 1973, is Norfolk & Western NW2 switcher No. 2018—originally Wabash No. 2806. In the distance is Chesapeake & Ohio GP7 road switcher No. 5774. *R. R. Richardson photo, Doug Eisele collection*

Opposite top: Western Pacific NW2 No. 608 rests at the Western Pacific Railroad Museum at Portola, California, on May 10, 2008. This model was Electro-Motive's standard 1,000-horsepower switcher and offered for 10 years beginning in 1939. Today, No. 608 is one of many preserved vintage diesels displayed at Portola. *Brian Solomon*

Opposite bottom: An Erie-Lackawanna NW2 rests outside of the former Erie Railroad shops at Hornell, New York, on February 13, 1973. Many railroads began dieselization with the acquisition of switchers in the 1930s and later sought road diesels during World War II. Erie was among the lines that bought Electro-Motive's FT for freight service during the war. *Doug Eisele*

In April 1991, two boys watch Southern Pacific SW1500 No. 2623 work industrial trackage on the Northwestern Pacific at Petaluma, California. SP was among the last railroads to order a large fleet of new switchers, and the railroad continued to encourage lineside carload traffic by building industrial parks along its lines into the 1970s. *Brian Solomon*

Southern Pacific's switchers were a common sight around its western system. In October 1990, SP SW1500 No. 2635 works the Cal-Train terminal at Seventh and King streets in San Francisco. SP remained the contract operator of San Francisco Peninsula "commute" trains until 1992 and thus continued to provide a San Francisco–based switcher at the passenger terminal. *Brian Solomon*

Southern Pacific was famous for its "full-house" lighting on diesel-electric locomotives. SP SW1500 No. 2530 features laterally mounted headlights (right), red oscillating lights on either side of the cab door, and a red warning oscillating light above the door. The red oscillating light would only be actuated in the event of a sudden loss of air-pipe pressure caused by an emergency airbrake application and was intended to warn other train crews that the train was in trouble and potentially derailed. *Brian Solomon*

The westbound *California Zephyr* makes its scheduled station stop at Denver Union Station in 1966 to pick up passengers and exchange the Burlington E-units that brought the train from Chicago with Rio Grande F7s for the trip over the Rockies. To the right of the *Zephyr* are a Rio Grande EMD SW1200 and a World War II–vintage Burlington Alco S-2 switcher. *Richard Jay Solomon*

Above: Wabash was a Midwestern railroad linking the gateway cities of Buffalo, Chicago, and Kansas City. Its main line between Buffalo/Niagara Falls and Detroit, Michigan, crossed Ontario, so Wabash had a fleet of Canadian-built F7As. Wabash's F7A No. 1189 has been preserved and restored by the Monticello Railway Museum at Monticello, Illinois. *Brian Solomon*

Left: Electro-Motive's distinctive styling gave its locomotives a modern streamlined appearance. This unusual angle looks down on the nose of privately owned former Alaska Railroad F7A No. 1508, working on the Adirondack Scenic Railroad. *Brian Solomon*

Among the most unusual Electro-Motive units operated by Rock Island were the streamlined LWT12 locomotive power cars for the lightweight trains built in the mid-1950s. Seen here is Rock Island's lone TALGO train built for the Rock's *Jet Rocket*. Electro-Motive built only three LWT12 locomotives; the other two powered General Motors' *Aerotrains*, which tested on the Pennsylvania Railroad, New York Central, and Union Pacific before being sold to the Rock. *Richard Jay Solomon*

The beautiful and the ugly posed nose to nose: Rock Island F-unit No. 310 and BL2 No. 425 face each other at Blue Island on July 18, 1958. In the late 1940s, Electro-Motive followed the lead established by Alco and introduced this 1,500-horsepower road-switcher model. The odd-looking BL1/BL2 was essentially an F3A in a modified carbody better suited for switching. *Richard Jay Solomon*

Few were the number of Electro-Motive BL2s—only 52 were built between 1947 and 1948—yet this unusual model found a great variety of work, from hauling potatoes in northern Maine to working branch lines in the Midwest and serving Rock Island in commuter service. At the end of a Chicago suburban run, Rock Island BL2 No. 429 rests at the Blue Island on July 18, 1958. *Richard Jay Solomon*

New Haven Railroad FL9s Nos. 2008 and 2012 race through South Norwalk working toward New Haven, Connecticut, on July 1963. New Haven's dual-mode FL9s were largely assigned to Boston–New York trains to eliminate the need for engine changes where steam or diesel power was exchanged for electric. *Richard Jay Solomon*

New Haven FL9s at Cos Cob on June 27, 1959. Electro-Motive's FL9 was a unique design, with specifications carefully tailored for New Haven's unusual service requirements. Among its unusual features was its dual-mode propulsion that allowed it to work as a diesel-electric or to draw power from the lineside third rail. *Richard Jay Solomon*

Repainted New Haven Railroad FL9 is seen with Waterbury, Connecticut, station's famous clock tower. In the 1980s, the Connecticut Department of Transportation paid to have four FL9s rebuilt and restored into their original New Haven livery for work on Connecticut branch trains. *Brian Solomon*

After Penn Central assumed operation of the New Haven Railroad in 1969, the FL9 fleet was largely reassigned to work suburban services on former New York Central lines out of Grand Central Terminal. These continued in such services for the next three decades. Metro-North FL9 No. 2041 leads a push-pull consist northward on the Hudson Line at the Breakneck Ridge tunnels on June 15, 1997. *Brian Solomon*

One of the more unusual late-era applications for former New Haven FL9s has been for seasonal passenger services on the old Maine Central Rockland Branch between Rockland, Bath, and New Brunswick, Maine. Maine Eastern FL9 No. 489 goes for a spin on the turntable at Rockland, Maine, after completing its day's work. *Brian Solomon*

In August 2007, Maine Eastern's FL9 No. 489 leads the railroad's passenger train at the Rockland, Maine, terminal. This was one of several FL9s operated by Amtrak on its Empire Corridor trains through the mid-1990s. Amtrak required third rail–equipped diesels to operate into the New York City terminals via the Hudson River route, although in later years the locomotives rarely worked in their electric mode. *Brian Solomon*

In its heyday, St. Louis Union Station was a crossroads of commerce. On July 22, 1958, train No. 15, the *Zephyr-Rocket*, departs St. Louis behind a Burlington E7A. Electro-Motive's E7 was the bestselling passenger locomotive of the postwar era and was bought by many railroads to supplant aging Pacific-type steam locomotives on named passenger trains. *Richard Jay Solomon*

July 27, 1958, finds a classic lineup of vintage diesels at Cincinnati Union Terminal's engine house. This photo clearly demonstrates styling differences between Electro-Motive's early production E-unit design, which used a steeply angled slant nose, and the more familiar postwar "bulldog nose." From left to right: Louisville & Nashville E7A No. 791 (built in 1949); L&N E6A No. 771 (1942); Pennsylvania Railroad E7A No. 5873 (1949); and Cincinnati Union Terminal Lima-Hamilton 750-horsepower switcher No. 20. *Richard Jay Solomon*

A pair of Rock Island E7As lead one of the railroad's famous *Rocket* streamliners near Chicago in 1961. Rock Island didn't join Amtrak in 1971 and continued to operate a ragtag fleet of E-units in both suburban and long-distance passenger service until the mid-1970s. *Richard Jay Solomon*

A pair of Erie Lackawanna E8s labor toward Gulf Summit, New York, with an eastward freight in July 1973. After E-L discontinued long-distance passenger services, it reassigned its E-units to freight work. While these were well liked for flatland running in the Midwest, their high-speed gearing and A1A trucks were ill-suited to steep grades in the East. *Kenneth J. Buck*

Restored New York Central E8A No. 4080 is displayed at the Medina Railroad Museum at Medina, New York. It is one of two units at the museum painted in the classic New York Central lightening stripe scheme. Electro-Motive E-units represented the majority of the Central's long-distance passenger locomotives in the diesel era. *Brian Solomon*

In summer 1963, New York Central E8A No. 4052 and an E7B lead a passenger train northward (railroad direction west) along the Hudson River toward Albany below the famous Bear Mountain bridge. *Richard Jay Solomon*

Pennsylvania Railroad No. 5711 became Conrail No. 4021, one of three E8s used by Conrail for its business train. It was restored by Juniata Terminal into its 1950s scheme with its old Pennsy number. Here Pennsy E8As approach Keating, Pennsylvania, along the banks of the Susquehanna River on October 11, 2003. *Brian Solomon*

Pennsy E8A No. 5711 is near Renovo, Pennsylvania, on October 11, 2003. The Juniata-restored E8As make occasional appearances on former Pennsylvania Railroad lines. *Brian Solomon*

Introduced in 1949, Electro-Motive's E8 represented a substantial improvement over the E7. By using three-phase AC motor-operated appliances, the new model eliminated belt-driven exhaust fans and other appliances. With the addition of high-capacity steam generators, the E8 featured more effective train heating while engine output was boosted to 2,250 horsepower compared with the E7's 2,000 horsepower. *Brian Solomon*

Above: Chicago & North Western GP7s Nos. 4117 and 4141 lead the northward Jefferson Junction local toward Clyman Junction at Johnson Creek, Wisconsin, on April 19, 1995. Electro-Motive dabbled with road-switcher designs in the mid-1940s by building a handful of NW3s and NW5s and then brought out the short-lived BL2 in 1948. It was the GP7 of 1949 that properly introduced the "general purpose" road switcher to Electro-Motive's catalog. *Brian Solomon*

Opposite top: The GP7 was built in large numbers between 1949 and 1954, when the model was replaced by the more powerful, more reliable, and even more versatile GP9. At sunset on May 11, 1995, C&NW GP7s approach Clyman Junction, Wisconsin. By this time, these locomotives had more than 40 years service since leaving Electro-Motive's plant. *Brian Solomon*

Opposite bottom: Detail of C&NW GP7 No. 4174, one of several units built new for the Rock Island and acquired by C&NW in the early 1980s after Rock's demise. C&NW continued to use its classic herald up until its merger with Union Pacific in spring 1995. *Brian Solomon*

Above: Springfield Terminal No. 21 works the yard at Lawrence, Massachusetts, in June 1987. It was built in Canada for the Algoma Central in 1963 and later acquired by Maine Central, becoming its No. 450. Significantly, this was the very last GP9 built and was finished many years after Electro-Motive had supplanted the GP9 with more powerful four-motor models. *Brian Solomon*

Opposite top: Boston & Maine was among the first railroads to replace its early Electro-Motive diesels with the more reliable types offered in the mid-1950s. In 1957, it traded back its World War II–era FT fleet on new GP9s numbered 1700–1749. These units used some components recycled from the old FTs. Boston & Maine GP9 No. 1736 works a local freight in Somerville, Massachusetts, against the Boston skyline in August 1989. *Brian Solomon*

Opposite bottom: Guilford Rail System GP9 No. 45, lettered for Springfield Terminal, works a Connecticut River Line local freight at Keats Road south of Greenfield, Massachusetts, on October 18, 2004. Originally it was Boston & Maine No. 1703 (later 1803) built in 1957. The reliability and durability of Electro-Motive's general purpose diesels have given them unusually long lifespans, with some units working well into their fifth decade. *Brian Solomon*

Southern Pacific's early GP9s were painted in its very classy "Black Widow" freight livery. Notice the panel below the numberboards for easy access. SP used numberboards to display train numbers rather than locomotive numbers, as was typical on most other railroads. The train number denotes a specific service, while a locomotive number identifies the specific engine. *Bob Morris*

Southern Pacific GP9E No. 3842 and a pair of SD9Es lead a westward freight along the shore of California's San Pablo Bay at Pinole on April 18, 1993. In the 1970s, SP rebuilt many of its 567-powered GP and SD units, which allowed them to continue in revenue freight service into the 1990s. *Brian Solomon*

Southern Pacific No. 3821 is among GP9Es laying over at Watsonville Junction on SP's Coast Line. In addition to oscillating lights and fixed headlights, SP diesels typically featured classification lamps, although by the 1990s these had been blanked out. Class lamps had been necessary for the method of train movement authorization under the old timetable and train order rules. *Brian Solomon*

Central Vermont was among the last railroads in New England to entirely displace steam with diesels. Some GP9s that had worked alongside 2-8-0s survived into the early 1990s. GP9s work at Dublin Street in Palmer, Massachusetts, in December 1988. Leading local freight No. 562 is CV No. 4549 and Grand Trunk No. 4139. *Brian Solomon*

Left: CV's pair of recently rebuilt GP9s (with low short hoods) works in fresh paint near the Hospital Road crossing in Monson, Massachusetts, on December 31, 1986. *Brian Solomon*

Opposite: CV was among several railroads that traditionally designated the long hood as front. While this offered increased safety for the crew, it reduced visibility. In the mid-1980s, Central Vermont rebuilt and lowered the short hood on two of its 1950s-built GP9s, resulting in the short end becoming the front. CV No. 4559 is seen at the Dublin Street engine facility in Palmer, Massachusetts. *Brian Solomon*

At 8:16 a.m., on July 14, 1988, Central Vermont No. 4926 is one of a sextet of GP9s leading southward freight No. 444 near Leverett, Massachusetts. The roar of classic 16-567 diesels could be heard for miles. *Brian Solomon*

Left: Central Vermont GP9 No. 4925 rests in the yard at Palmer alongside a Grand Trunk GP38. In the late 1980s and early 1990s, GP38s gradually replaced CV's aging fleet of GP9s. *Brian Solomon*

Below: Central Vermont's regular road freight operated six days a week between St. Albans, Vermont, and Palmer, Massachusetts. On July 2, 1988, five GP9s lead freight No. 444 across the Connecticut River bridge at East Northfield, Massachusetts. A speed restriction on the bridge insured the train crawled across the early twentieth-century span at 10 miles per hour. *Brian Solomon*

Southern Pacific GP20E No. 4112 leads the Woodland turn at Davis, California, in October 1989. The GP20 was Electro-Motive's early effort at producing a high-output four-motor road switcher, but it was known for turbocharger difficulties. Southern Pacific extended the life of its GP20 fleet by replacing the turbocharger with a more reliable method of engine aspiration. *Brian Solomon*

Under the gloom of a December sky, Toledo, Peoria & Western GP20s lead grain cars near Peoria, Illinois. No. 2015 wears a paint scheme inspired by the New York Central lightning stripe and adapted for TP&W by artist Mike Danneman. *Brian Solomon*

Wisconsin & Southern acquired a variety of EMD road switchers from Southern Pacific, including this old GP20E, originally SP No. 7224. Known by reporting marks WSOR, the railroad operated a network of lines in southern Wisconsin. On March 22, 1996, WSOR No. 4118 leads a freight over Wisconsin Central trackage in Waukesha. *Brian Solomon*

Although unremarkable when new, Electro-Motive's three GP18s built for New York, Susquehanna & Western in 1962 became one of the longest surviving original fleets. As late as autumn 2009, No. 1802 was still in service for the company. In October 1963, No. 1804 was working a freight in New Jersey. *Richard Jay Solomon*

Left: The application of a General Electric speedometer on this Electro-Motive-built NYS&W GP18 No. 1802 is confusing for casual observers. *Brian Solomon*

Opposite: NYS&W's GP18s were built with low short hoods. Other railroads, such as Rock Island and Norfolk & Western, bought GP18s with high short hoods. *Brian Solomon*

On July 3, 1989, a venerable Norfolk & Western high-hood GP30 leads a westward Norfolk Southern freight at Buffalo, New York. In the distance is the famous Buffalo Terminal. N&W and Southern were the only two railroads to order GP30s with the high short-hood option. *Brian Solomon*

In August 1998, former Rio Grande GP30 No. 3002 works a Union Pacific local freight at Antonito, Colorado. Rio Grande's GP30s were bought for fast freight service but ended up in slow-speed local service late in their careers. *Brian Solomon*

On March 12, 1980, Conrail GP30 No. 2247—still wearing Penn Central black—leads a freight at Overview, Pennsylvania, heading into the former Pennsylvania Railroad Enola Yard. The GP30 was powered by a 16-cylinder turbocharged 567 diesel. Turbocharging helped extract 2,250 horsepower from the 16-567, originally designed for 1,350-horsepower. *Doug Eisele*

In November 1988, a GP30 in fresh CSX paint leads a Chessie System GP40 westward over the Niagara Gorge at Niagara Falls, New York, with a Buffalo–Detroit freight. CSX's service on this route was inherited from the old Pere Marquette, a company acquired by CSX predecessor Chesapeake & Ohio in the 1940s. *Brian Solomon*

On October 4, 1984, Chesapeake & Ohio GP30 No. 3007, painted in the 1970s-inspired Chessie System livery, leads a GP9 off the former Buffalo, Rochester & Pittsburgh Belt Line on the way back to Brooks Avenue Yard in Rochester, New York. *Doug Eisele*

CSX predecessors Baltimore & Ohio and Chesapeake & Ohio both acquired large numbers of GP30s. CSX GP30 No. 4226 had been C&O No. 3035. It was among the first diesels painted in the CSX blue and gray livery. During the 1980s, many CSX GP30s were rebuilt and redesignated GP30Ms. Although CSX retired its last GP30 in 1997, some of the locomotives have been converted into road slugs (traction motors with ballast but no engine). *Brian Solomon*

In February 1995, New England Central assumed operations formerly handled by Canadian National Railway's Central Vermont subsidiary. GP38s 3850 and 3854 lead southward freight 608 past old mill buildings in Stafford Springs, Connecticut, in April 1998. *Brian Solomon*

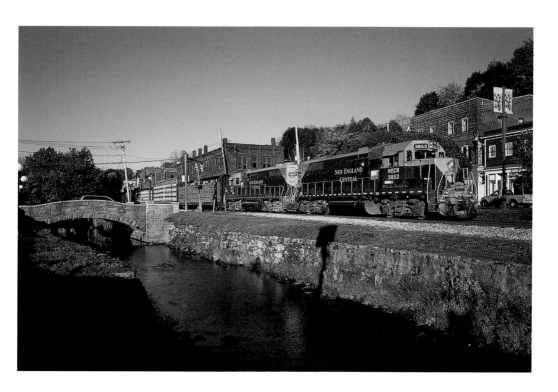

On October 13, 2006, New England Central GP38s Nos. 3853 and 3847 lead southward freight No. 608 through downtown Stafford Springs, Connecticut. New England Central serves local freight customers in southern New England and provides a through-service connection to Providence & Worcester in Connecticut. *Brian Solomon*

Approaching Belchertown, Massachusetts, in October 1998, New England Central engineer Steve Carlson works the throttle on a GP38. The 2,000-horsepower locomotive was well suited to the railroad's freight operations. *Brian Solomon*

Above: In 1972, Electro-Motive introduced its much-improved Dash 2 line that improved the electrical system used on its 645-series diesels. Most new models had the same output but offered a more reliable locomotive. The GP38-2 has remained as one of the most desirable locomotives for light freight service in North America. Wisconsin & Southern GP38-2 No. 3805 was photographed at Janesville, Wisconsin, in July 2005. *Brian Solomon*

Opposite top: Delaware & Hudson GP38s Nos. 7312 and 7304 work a local freight along the old Erie Railroad main line at Owego, New York, in October 2002. CP Rail acquired the old D&H in 1990, and these locomotives were retroactively painted into the D&H "heritage livery," originally introduced on the four Alco PA cab units D&H acquired from Santa Fe in the 1960s. *Brian Solomon*

Opposite bottom: Pittsburgh & Lake Erie GP38-2s leading a loaded Bow coal train at William Street in Buffalo. The train has just come in on Norfolk Southern's former Nickel Plate Road route and waits for a D&H crew to take it east on the old Erie Railroad. *Brian Solomon*

In June 1994, Southern Pacific SD9E No. 4411 leads a work train over Pengra Pass in the Oregon Cascades. SP bought 149 SD9s—the majority of Electro-Motive's production. Many served the railroad for the better part of four decades; most were rebuilt in-kind as SD9Es in the 1970s to extend their service lives. *Brian Solomon*

Above: In May 1990, a pair of SP SD9 "Cadillacs" catches the evening light at Grants Pass, Oregon. These smooth-riding units were regulars on the Medford–Grants Pass turn in the early 1990s before SP discontinued operations on the Siskiyou Line and sold the route to RailTex. *Brian Solomon*

Opposite: This closeup of SP SD9E No. 4372 finds it equipped with the classic SP full-lighting arrangement that includes oscillating headlights, sealed-beam headlights, and classification lamps. *Brian Solomon*

Above: Duluth, Missabe & Iron Range SD9 No. 166 was still wearing factory paint when it rested at the Wisconsin Central shops in North Fond du Lac, Wisconsin, on September 2, 1995. Ore-hauling DM&IR was a natural customer for high-tractive-effort six-motor diesels, which replaced its massive 2-8-8-4 Yellowstones in the 1950s. *Brian Solomon*

Opposite top: Chicago & North Western SD9 No. 1703 rests in Chicago near a steam-era coaling tower on July 17, 1958. "Route of the Streamliners" dates from the time when C&NW forwarded Union Pacific's famous trains from Omaha to Chicago. *Richard Jay Solomon*

Opposite bottom: On September 23, 1994, Burlington Northern SD9 No. 6150 leads a local freight at Gunn, Minnesota. In essence, Electro-Motive's SD9 was a six-motor variation of the popular GP9. Both models shared many of the same mechanical and electrical components with the obvious exception of the trucks. *Brian Solomon*

Wisconsin Central F45 No. 6651 and FP45 No. 6652 work freight No. 119 from North Fond du Lac to Green Bay, Wisconsin, at Kaukauna on April 6, 1996. Wisconsin Central acquired a handful of F45s and a sole FP45 from Santa Fe in the mid-1990s. *Brian Solomon*

Train 348 roars through Waukesha, Wisconsin, on March 22, 1996, with Wisconsin Central F45 No. 6655 in the lead on a bright, sunny day. What better reason to escape the office than to watch a freshly painted F45 roll through town? *Brian Solomon*

On May 4, 1996, Wisconsin Central F45 No. 6656 was displayed for public viewing on the East Troy Electric at Mukwonago, Wisconsin. Wisconsin Central—along with Montana Rail Link; New York, Susquehanna & Western; and Wisconsin & Southern—operated F45s acquired secondhand after Electro-Motive's 20-cylinder 645E3 prime mover had largely fallen out of favor on the larger railroads. *Brian Solomon*

New Santa Fe FP45s Nos. 105 and 104 lead the *El Capitan* in 1968. Powered by the 3,600-horsepower 20-cylinder 645E3 engine, these were among the most powerful single-unit passenger diesels of the 1960s. *Richard Jay Solomon*

Wisconsin Central FP45 No. 6652 still wears Santa Fe warbonnet paint. On September 2, 1995, it was photographed alongside WC's Algoma Central FP9 No. 1752 at North Fond du Lac shops. *Brian Solomon*

Opposite: The popular Santa Fe FP45 No. 92 is now displayed at the Illinois Railway Museum in Union, Illinois. Built in 1967 as Santa Fe No. 102, this locomotive enjoyed a 30-year career hauling passenger and freight trains before being preserved at IRM in 1997. *Brian Solomon*

Left: In the mid-1960s, Electro-Motive met Santa Fe's request for a shrouded diesel by adapting the SD45 with external cowling that shrouded the machinery. Unlike the old E- and F-units, whose carbodies were integral to their structure, the shrouds of cowl-type locomotives are non-integral. This is a windshield detail of Santa Fe F45 No. 5959. *Brian Solomon*

Below: The success of the FP45 led Santa Fe and the Great Northern to order 20-cylinder F45s solely for freight service. These looked very similar and shared most components with the FP45 designed for passenger and freight service. *Brian Solomon*

Santa Fe continued to operate its F45/FP45 fleet into the 1990s. When Santa Fe began to pare down its roster of 20-cylinder diesels, including its SD45s, it sold some F45s and one FP45 to Wisconsin Central. *Brian Solomon*

At 2:20 p.m. on January 22, 1991, Santa Fe SD45 No. 5400 storms westward at Bagdad, California, on Santa Fe's Needles District in the Mojave Desert. Electro-Motive's 20-cylinder diesels, including the SD45, F45, and SD45-2, had a distinctive, low throbbing sound that could be heard for many miles. *Brian Solomon*

Above: On June 22, 1982, Rio Grande SD45 No. 5336 and a pair of Union Pacific SD45s lead a westward Rio Grande coal train. While Rio Grande's SD45 fleet was among the longest to survive, UP's was one of the shortest. *George W. Kowanski*

Opposite: New York, Susquehanna & Western SD45 No. 3620 reveals its Burlington Northern heritage with a bit of cascade green paint visible atop the short hood. Susquehanna acquired a small fleet of former BN SD45s and F45s in the late 1980s for use on its transcontinental Sea-Land double-stack container trains. *Brian Solomon*

On December 3, 1994, Wisconsin Central SD45s ascend Byron Hill at Lost Arrow Road a few miles south of Fond du Lac, Wisconsin. For several years after Wisconsin Central was acquired by Canadian National in 2001, the railroad continued to operate SD45s in road-freight service; Byron Hill was among the last places to hear multiple SD45s hard at work, their 20-645E3 engines resonating across cornfields. *Brian Solomon*

The SD45 was visually distinguishable from other EMD six-motor road switchers by its diagonally oriented or "flared" radiator intake arrangement. WC No. 6593 is shown here at Byron, Wisconsin, on the morning of April 6, 1996. *Brian Solomon*

Wisconsin Central SD45s cross-plowed cornfields south of Byron, Wisconsin, on their way from the yards at North Fond du Lac to Chicago. WC's secondhand SD45 fleet was one of the last big fleets of 20-cylinder diesels in the United States. *Brian Solomon*

Chapter 4

Fairbanks-Morse

Fairbanks-Morse

Fairbanks-Morse's railroad connections date to the late nineteenth century. Early F-M railroad products consisted of track-maintenance equipment, including work cars, velocipedes, and handcars with the familiar walking-beam power lever. By 1893, F-M was selling gasoline engines for railcars, and in the early twentieth century it was building gasoline-powered railcars and small industrial gasoline-mechanical locomotives.

During the 1930s, F-M was one of several companies that benefited from research and development of compact high-output diesels for naval applications. This program resulted in F-M's unusual two-cycle opposed-piston engine. Each cylinder served a pair of pistons facing one another, obviating the need for cylinder heads, requiring fewer moving parts, and benefiting from superior heat dissipation while operating with lower piston speeds.

By 1940, F-M was the second-largest diesel engine-builder in the United States, and during World War II it provided large numbers of engines for submarines and other military applications. To accommodate its booming production, F-M greatly expanded its capacity, particularly at its Beloit,

Wisconsin, factory. In mid-1944, it entered the heavy domestic locomotive business. The War Production Board initially limited F-M to switchers, but after the war the company introduced a complete line of locomotives with configurations comparable to other builders. In several instances, F-M's offerings were significantly more powerful than competitors'. All of these locomotives were powered by variations of F-M's successful 38D8-1/8 opposed-piston design, which it manufactured in 6-, 8-, 10- and 12-cylinder varieties.

Most F-M locomotives for the domestic market were built at its Beloit plant. An exception were its first carbody types, large road diesels built between 1945 and 1949, which used bodies erected under contract by General Electric at Erie, Pennsylvania. To serve the Canadian market, F-M licensed its locomotive designs to the Canadian Locomotive Company of Kingston, Ontario.

As with the other large builders, F-M started with a moderately powered switcher, the H-10-44 (H for hood, 10 for 1,000 horsepower, and 44 for four axles and four motors), and then introduced a host of road types. Initially it offered road switchers in two four-motor varieties: the 1,500-horsepower H-15-44 and 2,000-horsepower H-20-44. The latter model was peculiar, as it featured an end-cab design more typical of slow-geared switchers but was equipped with road trucks geared for 65 miles per hour (this was the most powerful road switcher at the time). This type remained relatively obscure and was only ordered by five railroads with less than 100 units built.

F-M's initial streamlined road diesels were the aforementioned Erie-built models. These were rated at 2,000 horsepower and powered by the same 10-cylinder opposed-piston engine used in the H-20-44. In 1950, F-M introduced its much improved Consolidation line (known popularly as C-Liners). These streamlined carbody diesels were available in 11 different configurations, ranging from 1,600 to 2,400 horsepower per unit. Although similar to the Erie-built units in general appearance, they embraced a more refined exterior design. At the same time, F-M also increased its standard four-motor road switcher from 1,500 to 1,600 horsepower, a move equivalent with Alco and

Baldwin improvements implemented about the same time. In 1951, F-M introduced the H-16-66 six-motor road switcher. This was supplemented in 1953 by the famed Train-Master H-24-66, a large and very powerful six-motor type rated at 2,400 horsepower per unit. Although only 127 units were sold, it was F-M's most influential model and set a high-horsepower precedent emulated more successfully by Alco, Electro-Motive, and General Electric.

F-M sold 1,256 diesel-electric locomotives, yet was the least successful of the four large diesel locomotive builders in the postwar period. It consistently held fourth place in market share until 1953, when it finally passed Baldwin. While F-M built locomotives until 1963, the vast majority of its domestic production was conducted in its first decade as a builder and it sold very few locomotives after 1957.

F-M diesels tended not to fair well on railroads that mixed F-Ms into road pools with minimal concern for their more specialized service requirements. By the mid-1960s, unmodified F-M diesels were already rare. Most were retired by the mid-1970s.

Previous pages:
Long Island Rail Road C-Liner No. 2006 basks in the evening sun on November 6, 1960, at Montauk Point, New York. The Fairbanks-Morse CPA-20-5 used an unusual B-A1A wheel arrangement to provide added support for a steam boiler at the rear of the locomotive while keeping axle weight within acceptable limits. *Richard Jay Solomon*

Pittsburgh & Lake Erie affiliate Pittsburgh, Chartiers & Youghiogheny Railway operated this orphan 1,000-horsepower F-M switcher that it purchased in 1949. PC&Y No. 1 was stored among Alcos at P&LE's shops at McKees Rocks, Pennsylvania, on July 9, 1958. *Richard Jay Solomon*

Above: Dressed to represent Southern Pacific No. 1487, complete with large oscillating headlight, this F-M H-12-44 switcher is former U.S. Army No. 1874. In October 2003, it was photographed at the Golden Gate Railway Museum at Hunters Point in San Francisco. Today, it resides with the GGRM collection at Brightside in California's Niles Canyon. *Brian Solomon*

Opposite: This interior view of the cab of former Milwaukee Road F-M H-10-44 No. 767 shows the arrangement of the control stand. Built at Beloit, Wisconsin, No. 767 is preserved in working condition at the National Railroad Museum in Green Bay, Wisconsin. Only a handful of F-M diesels have been preserved. *Brian Solomon*

Central Railroad of New Jersey, which operated one of the most eclectic diesel fleets in the United States, had several F-M models. In June 1961, CNJ H-15-44 No. 1508 leads a Jersey City–bound commuter train across the massive Newark Bay bridge at Bayonne, New Jersey. *Richard Jay Solomon*

Central Railroad of New Jersey F-M H-15-44 No. 1514 switches a suburban train at Communipaw Yards in Jersey City on April 24, 1958. At the time, some photographers may have considered the row of automobiles in the foreground an annoyance, but today they are as interesting as the curious opposed-piston diesel-electric. *Richard Jay Solomon*

Fairbanks-Morse locomotives abound in this classic photo at Jersey City on the afternoon of August 25, 1959. On the left, Central Railroad of New Jersey H-15-44 No. 1512 switches a Reading Company train, while an H-24-66 Train-Master roars out of CNJ's terminal station with a commuter train. Another F-M can be seen lurking under the train shed. *Richard Jay Solomon*

Above: Pittsburgh & West Virginia was one of only a few railroads that preferred F-M diesels over other manufacturers and in the 1950s made its transition from steam power to two-cycle opposed-piston diesels. P&WV H-20-44s Nos. 55 and 63 are shown at Rook, Pennsylvania, in 1958. Norfolk & Western absorbed the operations of P&WV in 1964. *Richard Jay Solomon*

Opposite top: By the mid-1950s, the versatility of the diesel-electric road switcher had made it the predominant type of new locomotive. P&WV H16-44 No. 91 pauses on the turntable at Rook, near Pittsburgh, Pennsylvania. This locomotive was not yet two years old when seen on July 6, 1958. Bidirectional road switchers rendered turning facilities unnecessary and simplified operations. *Richard Jay Solomon*

Opposite bottom: A pair of P&WV H-20-44s leads train 92 at Rook on July 6, 1958. P&WV's 12 H-20-44s were numbered 50–71. F-M built just 96 H-20-44s between 1947 and 1954, and P&WV was among only five railroads to purchase this unusually powerful four-motor model. Although they feature the end-cab design typically associated with low-speed switchers, the H-20-44 was geared for road service. *Richard Jay Solomon*

Above: Akron, Canton & Youngstown was an unusual industrial short line because the majority of its diesel fleet consisted of F-M road switchers, including H-16-44s (pictured), a few H-20-44s, but also a few Alco S-2s and a sole Alco RS-1. *J. William Vigrass*

Opposite top: A New Haven Railroad F-M H-16-44 road switcher and a GP9 lead a work train at Eastchester Bay, New York, on June 27, 1959. New Haven's early approach to dieselization was unusual: It bought diesels from every builder except Electro-Motive. New Haven operated several F-M models, including these road switchers. It wasn't until the mid-1950s that NH bought Electro-Motive diesels, including the custom-designed FL9s. *Richard Jay Solomon*

Opposite bottom: On July 24, 1958, Southern Railway H-16-44 No. 2148 leads a short local freight through Centralia, Illinois. F-M diesels were unusual on the Southern. It owned just 10 H-16-44s, although its Cincinnati, New Orleans & Texas Pacific subsidiary also owned some, along with a rarely photographed fleet of H-24-66 Train-Masters. *Richard Jay Solomon*

Central Railroad of New Jersey F-M Train-Master No. 2404 leads a Canadian Pacific 4-6-2 on an excursion in eastern Pennsylvania in October 1966. While most fans at the time were probably enthralled by the steam locomotive, it is the H-24-66 that is of greater interest today. The steam engine is still with us, while the F-M was cut up for scrap decades ago. *Richard Jay Solomon*

In July 1964, Central Railroad of New Jersey H-24-66 No. 2410 leads a three-car suburban train on the New York & Long Branch. Both Pennsylvania Railroad and CNJ provided suburban services on the NY&LB, and in the mid-1960s this route was a bastion of unusual and eclectic diesel power. Today, NJ Transit provides passenger services on the line. *Richard Jay Solomon*

Central Railroad of New Jersey, along with Southern Pacific, assigned 2,400-horsepower F-M Train-Masters to suburban passenger services where frequent stops meant that locomotives needed to get up to speed quickly to maintain schedules. *Richard Jay Solomon*

An A-B-B-A set of New York Central's Fairbanks-Morse CFA-20-4 C-Liners roar eastbound through the deep cut east of Washington Station, Massachusetts, on the old Boston & Albany route on August 22, 1954. Leading is No. 5004. The Central bought several C-Liner models in the early 1950s, but the locomotives remained relatively obscure among the hoards of Electro-Motives and Alcos. *Robert A. Buck*

New York Central C-Liners Nos. 5007 and 5009 work east at Tower SM at the east end of the enormous Alfred H. Smith Memorial Bridge across the Hudson Valley at Castleton, New York, on August 22, 1954. For a few years from the late-1940s through the mid-1950s, F-M diesels were commonly assigned to the Boston & Albany route. *Robert A. Buck*

This nose view shows New York Central C-Liner No. 6603 as it looked in the late-era "cigar band" livery. Built in 1952, this was one of seven CFA-16-4 models built for Central. Where Central's 5000-series CFA-20-4s were rated at 2,000 horsepower per unit, these similar-looking C-Liners were rated at just 1,600 horsepower. In 1960, Electro-Motive rebuilt these C-Liners by replacing the F-M diesels with their own engines. *Jim Shaughnessy*

Milwaukee Road ordered 15 powerful Fairbanks-Morse "Erie-builts" for service on its *Olympian Hiawatha*. They were assembled at GE's Erie, Pennsylvania, plant between December 1945 and March 1947, and they originally were adorned with an attractive stainless-steel styling on the nose. All the Erie-built locomotives rode on A1A trucks and were powered by Fairbanks-Morse's 2,000-horsepower 10-cylinder opposed-piston diesel. No. 12A is shown at Chicago's Western Avenue Yard on July 17, 1958. *Richard Jay Solomon*

A Canadian National C-Liner rests among a variety of other diesels and stored steam locomotives at Montreal's Turcot Yards on May 4, 1958. F-M's locomotives for the Canadian market were assembled by the Canadian Locomotive Company at Kingston, Ontario. Canadian National and Canadian Pacific both bought C-Liners and F-M road switchers. *Richard Jay Solomon*

A pair of New York Central C-Liners work eastward through Warren, Massachusetts, on a lovely autumn morning in the early 1950s. *Warren St. George photo, courtesy of Robert A. Buck*

Chapter 5
General Electric

General Electric

Beginning in the 1890s, General Electric was among the pioneers in the development of heavy electric locomotives and related technology. In the early years of the twentieth century, GE built gas-electric railcars and dabbled in gas-electric locomotives. During the World War I period, GE attempted to construct small diesel-electrics but gave up before achieving commercial success. Then, in the mid-1920s, GE entered a consortium with Alco and Ingersoll-Rand in the production of small diesel-electric switchers that are generally regarded as the world's first commercially successful diesel locomotives. It might seem strange that despite GE's important achievements in the formative years of diesel development, it opted to remain largely a supplier and contract producer of diesel electric technology during the crucial changeover period from steam to diesel. Yet, its roll as Alco's partner between 1940 and 1953 gave GE a satisfactory level of design control in the construction of diesels. These locomotives were jointly marketed as Alco-GE products but constructed by Alco at Schenectady, New York.

During this period, GE did manufacture a line of small switchers designed for industrial, yard, and branch-line applications at its own Schenectady plant. Best known of these were its 44-ton center cab, intended for one-man operation on common carrier railroads, and an end-cab 70-ton model. During this same time period, GE continued to build heavy straight electrics and gas-turbine electric road locomotives at its Erie, Pennsylvania, plant. Interestingly, GE's heavy electrics and turbines shared styling similarities with the Alco FA/PA diesels as a result of GE providing industrial design for Alco's road diesel carbodies.

It was logical for GE to develop its own line of heavy road diesels after it parted ways with Alco in 1953, and during the mid-1950s GE quietly worked at research and development of high-horsepower locomotives. It bought the Cooper-Bessemer FDL diesel design and adapted it for high-output locomotive service. Initially, GE focused its road diesel types on the export market, but in 1959 and 1960, it debuted its Universal Series for domestic applications. First was its famed U25B, a four-motor

2,500-horsepower road-switcher type aimed at fast freight service. At the time of its introduction, this was the most powerful single-unit diesel-electric on the domestic market, and it offered serious competition to models built by Alco and EMD (by that time Baldwin and Fairbanks-Morse had exited the domestic locomotive market). In 1963, GE introduced a six-motor model called the U25C. GE soon claimed the position of second-most productive diesel locomotive manufacturer, edging out its one-time partner.

During the 1960s, many railroads were replacing postwar diesels with more powerful and more reliable locomotives. Part of this strategy was buying new units that would do the same work as two of the older units, and all of the manufacturers gradually increased the output of their standard models. When in the mid-1960s Alco and EMD matched the output of their products to meet or exceed that of GE, the latter introduced new, more powerful models. In late 1965 and early 1966, GE introduced new 2,800-horsepower units to supplant its 2,500-horsepower units. Then, a year later, it introduced 3,000-horsepower models, matching the output then offered by Electro-Motive's GP40 and SD40. GE's U30C proved to be its most successful U model with nearly 600 units sold to domestic lines. While 3,000-horsepower models remained in production through the mid-1970s, GE also offered 3,300-horsepower and 3,600-horsepower road freight types: models U33C and U36C that competed with Alco's C-636 and Electro-Motive's successful SD45, as well as U33B and U36B four-motor types.

While General Electric initially addressed the most lucrative segment of the American locomotive market—road freight locomotives—on request of customers, it adapted its Universal designs for passenger applications, notably building U28CG and U30CG models for Santa Fe with steam generators and U34CH with head-end power capabilities for Erie-Lackawanna.

Although in the 1960s and 1970s, high-horsepower locomotives drew a significant demand, some railroads still required locomotives of more nominal output. For these applications, GE offered the four-motor U23B and six-motor U23C, both rated at 2,250 horsepower. The U23B, which remained in production until 1977, sold 425 units domestically, making it the second-most common four-motor U-boat.

Previous pages:
Delaware & Hudson bought a variety of General Electric's Universal Series diesels. On October 13, 1976, D&H U30C No. 712 and a pair of U33Cs work eastward with freight NE-2 at Maryland, New York. *George W. Kowanski*

Above: New Hampshire–based Claremont & Concord traditionally operated remnants of a light Boston & Maine branch and portions of a one-time electric interurban line in the vicinity of Claremont, New Hampshire. *Jim Shaughnessy*

Opposite top: Middletown & New Jersey GE 44-ton switcher No. 1 leads an excursion in September 1962. This 380-horsepower switcher was built for the Middletown & Unionville. Typical of lightweight GE switchers, it was designed for one-man operation. *Richard Jay Solomon*

Opposite bottom: The lateral symmetry and balanced designed of GE's 44-ton diesels is anomalous in American practice, where diesel locomotives have tended to use off-center designs. Restored Pennsylvania Railroad GE 44-ton switcher No. 9331 is at Strasburg, Pennsylvania. *Brian Solomon*

Above: General Electric's initial entry into the domestic heavy road-switcher market was its famed U25B. At the time of its debut in 1959, the 2,500-horsepower U25B was the most powerful single-engine diesel-electric in the United States and designed for fast freight service. Chesapeake & Ohio U25B No. 2528 rests at Sloan, New York, in December 1968. *Doug Eisele*

Left: Southern Pacific U25B No. 3100 was built by General Electric in 1963 as SP No. 7508, one of 68 U25Bs ultimately operated by SP. In their heyday, SP's U25Bs were assigned primarily to road freights east of Los Angeles on the Sunset Route. No. 3100 is seen here at the Orange Empire Railway Museum near Perris, California. *Brian Solomon*

Conrail U25B No. 2612 and two other Universal Series GE "U-boats" lead a freight across the Susquehanna River on the famous Rockville bridge on October 20, 1979. Conrail operated one of the largest rosters of U-boats, inheriting a variety of models from its predecessors and buying locomotives new from GE in the mid-1970s. After GE phased out its U-boat line, Conrail remained one of its better customers and acquired large numbers Dash 7 and Dash 8 models. *Doug Eisele*

Above: Erie Lackawanna operations on the old Erie main line were conducive to high-horsepower road switchers, and in the 1960s EL turned to all three remaining builders for powerful diesels, including U25B No. 2502, shown at Port Jervis, New York, in October 1974. *George W. Kowanski*

Opposite top: Erie Lackawanna U25Bs Nos. 2507 and 2518 lead a short westward freight through the crossovers at East Hornell, New York, on October 27, 1975. This train has just sprinted up the famed Canisteo River Valley, a remote and exceptionally scenic location that had served the old Erie as conduit of commerce since the 1850s. *Bill Dechau photo, Doug Eisele collection*

Opposite bottom: Erie Lackawanna U25B No. 2513 is seen at Hornell, New York, on September 21, 1975. Hornell owed its prosperity to the Erie Railroad, which located locomotive shops, divisional offices, dispatchers, and freight yards around the town. The downgrading of the old Erie route following the creation of Conrail in 1976 hasn't been kind to communities such as Hornell, their heydays long since past. *Doug Eisele*

Above: Conrail U23B No. 2797 leads an eastward freight at Rotterdam Junction New York in June 1989. Sister locomotive, Conrail No. 2798, was the last domestic U-boat built and has been preserved in working order on the Naugatuck Railroad in Connecticut. *Brian Solomon*

Opposite top: In the 1960s and 1970s, Delaware & Hudson looked to both Alco and GE for new high-horsepower units. However, not all its new diesels were high-output models. It bought the more moderately powered U23B for road service as well. On September 12, 1982, a trio of GE U23Bs, led by No. 2304, works a westward freight at Big Flats, New York, on the former Erie Railroad main line. As a condition of the creation of Conrail, D&H was granted trackage rights on the old Erie between Binghamton and Buffalo, New York. *Doug Eisele*

Opposite bottom: Penn Central U23B No. 2740 kicks up the snow as it works east on the former New York Central Water Level Route near East Rochester, New York, on February 17, 1973. By the mid-1970s, the New York Central was primarily a heavy-freight corridor. *R. R. Richardson photo, Doug Eisele collection*

Above: Shortly after Lehigh Valley's U23Bs were delivered in radiant "Cornell red," Lehigh Valley was absorbed into Conrail. LV *Apollo-2* works east at Laurel Run, Pennsylvania. The Lehigh Valley route was one of several duplicate routes connecting the New York City metro area with the Niagara Frontier. Under Conrail, its route was truncated and much of it downgraded or abandoned. *George W. Kowanski*

Opposite top: Lehigh Valley's premier freight was its *Apollo* piggyback train. In March 1976, its eastward *Apollo-2* exits Pennsylvania's White Haven Tunnel behind new General Electric U23B No. 504. *George W. Kowanski*

Opposite bottom: Three clean Lehigh Valley U23Bs lead the *Apollo-2* eastbound at Phillipsburg, New Jersey. These moderately powered four-motor GE diesels were well suited to Lehigh Valley's graded operations. *George W. Kowanski*

Above: The merger of New York Central, the Pennsy, and the New Haven resulted in an eclectic mix of motive power, all of which was painted in Penn Central's dreary black livery. GE U30B No. 2865, Alco RS27 No. 2402, and a U25B haul an eastward freight east of Rochester, New York's Goodman Street Yard on March 12, 1974. *Bill Dechau photo, Doug Eisele collection*

Opposite top: The Penn Central bankruptcy ultimately resulted in the creation of Conrail. In August 1970, PC U33B No. 2895 and a GP38 lead a westward freight through the old Pennsylvania Railroad tunnels at Gallitzin. *George W. Kowanski*

Opposite bottom: GE's U30B matched Electro-Motive's GP40 in output but not reliability. On November 16, 1974, Penn Central U30B No. 2880, a U33B, and a U33C roar westward at Rochester, New York, with symbol freight VB-1. The Penn Central and these old GE diesels are all just a memory now. Today, CSX operates the old Water Level Route, largely with modern 4,400-horsepower GE diesels that are far more reliable than these beasts from the 1970s. *Doug Eisele*

Above: D&H U30C No. 712 leads eastward symbol freight NE2 over Richmondville Hill near Warnerville, New York, on October 13, 1976. D&H operated a fleet of six-motor GEs, including both U30Cs and U33Cs. *George W. Kowanski*

Opposite top: Boston & Maine joined Maine Central (MEC) under Guilford control in 1983. When Guilford acquired a group of secondhand SD40s and a sole U30C from Detroit Edison in the mid-1980s, it assigned the Electro-Motive units to MEC and the six-motor GE to B&M—an anomalous addition to B&M's otherwise four-motor fleet. *Brian Solomon*

Opposite bottom: On May 7, 1988, B&M U30C No. 663, former Detroit Edison No. 012, works eastward through the Canisteo Valley at Newcomb Road near Addison, New York, leading Delaware & Hudson symbol freight DHT-4. This Sealand container train utilized D&H trackage rights over Conrail's former Erie main lines between Buffalo and Binghamton in a complex arrangement that forwarded the containers to New Jersey for distribution. *Brian Solomon*

Above: Two Delaware & Hudson U33Cs bracket Maine Central U23B—formerly a D&H unit—on a westward freight approaching Dixons Crossing near Attica, New York. In 1976, D&H's trackage rights on Conrail's former Erie Railroad route between Binghamton and Buffalo boosted traffic on this orphaned route. *Brian Solomon*

Opposite top: In Conrail's early years, it operated a faded rainbow fleet of locomotives inherited from its predecessor lines. On August 20, 1977, a former Penn Central U33C leads a former Reading Company U30C west at Lincoln Park in Rochester, New York. *Doug Eisele*

Opposite bottom: On December 12, 1971, Erie Lackawanna U33C No. 3315 works west with two 20-cylinder EMDs on the old Erie Railroad main line near Waverly, New York. EL bought a variety of high-horsepower six-motor road switchers for road freight service to give it a competitive edge with its primary competitor, Penn Central. Yet, after EL was folded into Conrail in 1976, freight traffic was focused on former PC routes and much of the EL route was downgraded. *Bill Dechau, Doug Eisele*

EL acquired these big GE units specifically for suburban passenger work on nonelectrified routes radiating from Hoboken. In later years, NJ Transit inherited EL's units but continued to base them in Hoboken on former EL routes. NJ Transit U34CH No. 4167 rests between commuter runs on the former Erie at Suffern, New York, in March 1989. *Brian Solomon*

Erie Lackawanna was the only railroad to acquire GE's model U34CH. This passenger-service six-motor worked lines out of the former Lackawanna Terminal in Hoboken. In June 1971, EL No. 3359 was only a few months old when it led a westward suburban run on the old Erie Railroad main line at Waldwick, New Jersey. *George W. Kowanski*

Erie Lackawanna's 32 U34CH diesels were paid for by the New Jersey Department of Transportation and thus wore an unusual variation of the EL livery. These locomotives ultimately served NJ Transit, which assumed operations of commuter rail lines in the state in the early 1980s. The U34CH was a variation of the U36C with head-end power provisions for passenger-car heating and lighting. *George W. Kowanski*

BOOKS

Armstrong, John H. *The Railroad: What It Is, What It Does.* Omaha, Neb.: Simmons-Boardman Books, 1982.

Bush, Donald J. *The Streamlined Decade.* New York: Braziller, 1975.

Churella, Albert J. *From Steam to Diesel.* Princeton, N.J.: Princeton University Press, 1998.

Diesel Era. The Revolutionary Diesel: EMC's FT. Halifax, Pa.: Withers Publishing, 1994.

Diesel Locomotive Roster: The Railroad Magazine Series. New York: Wayner Publications, [no date].

Doherty, Timothy Scott, and Brian Solomon. *Conrail.* St. Paul, Minn.: MBI Publishing, 2004.

Dolzall, Gary W., and Stephen F. Dolzall. *Baldwin Diesel Locomotives.* Milwaukee, Wis.: Kalmbach Publishing, 1984.

———. *Monon: The Hoosier Line.* Glendale, Calif.: Interurban Press, 1987.

Draney, John. *Diesel Locomotives: Electrical Equipment.* Chicago: American Technical Society, 1948.

Edson, William D. with H. L. Vail Jr. and C. M. Smith. *New York Central Diesel Locomotives.* Lynchburg, Va.: TLC Publishing, 1995.

Farrington, S. Kip Jr. *Railroads at War.* New York: Coward-McCann, 1944.

———. *Railroading from the Rear End.* New York: Coward-McCann, 1946.

———. *Railroading the Modern Way.* New York: Coward-McCann, 1951.

Garmany, John B. *Southern Pacific Dieselization.* Edmonds, Wash.: Pacific Fast Mail, 1985.

Harlow, Alvin F. *The Road of the Century.* New York: Creative Age Press, 1947.

Hartley, Scott. *New England Alcos in Twilight.* Homewood, Ill.: PTJ Publishing, 1983.

Jennison, Brian, and Victor Neves. *Southern Pacific Oregon Division.* Mukilteo, Wash.: Hundman Publishing, 1997.

Jones, Robert C. *The Central Vermont Railway, Vol. VII.* Shelburne, Vt.: The New England Press, 1995.

Jones, Robert W. *Boston & Albany: The New York Central in New England, Vols. 1 & 2.* Los Angeles: Pine Tree Press, 1997.

Keilty, Edmund. *Interurbans without Wires.* Glendale, Calif.: Interurban Press, 1979.

Kiefer, P. W. *A Practical Evaluation of Railroad Motive Power.* New York: Simmons-Boardman Books, 1948.

Kirkland, John F. *The Diesel Builders Vols. I, II & III.* Glendale, Calif.: Interurban Press, 1983.

———*Dawn of the Diesel Age.* Pasadena, Calif.: Interurban Press, 1994.

Klein, Maury. *Union Pacific, Vols. I & II.* New York: Doubleday, 1989.

Lloyd, Gordon Jr., and Louis A. Marre. *Conrail Motive Power Review, Vol. 1.* Glendale, Calif.: Interurban Press, 1992.

Marre, Louis, A. *Diesel Locomotives: The First 50 Years.* Waukesha, Wis.: Kalmbach Publishing, 1995.

Marre, Louis A., and Jerry A. Pinkepank. *The Contemporary Diesel Spotter's Guide.* Milwaukee, Wis.: Kalmbach Publishing, 1985.

McDonald, Charles W. *Diesel Locomotive Rosters.* Milwaukee, Wis.: Kalmbach Publishing, 1982.

McDonnell, Greg. *U-Boats: General Electric Diesel Locomotives.* Toronto: Boston Mills Press, 1994.

McMillan, Joe. *Santa Fe's Diesel Fleet.* Burlingame, Calif.: Chatham Publishing, 1975.

Middleton, William D. *When the Steam Railroads Electrified.* Milwaukee, Wis.: Kalmbach Publishing, 1974.

Mulhearn, Daniel J., and John R. Taibi. *General Motors' F-Units.* New York: Quadrant Press, 1982.

Nowak, Ed. *Ed Nowak's New York Central.* Park Forest, Ill.: PTJ Publishing, 1983.

Pinkepank, Jerry A. *The Diesel Spotter's Guide.* Milwaukee, Wis.: Kalmbach Publishing, 1967.

———. *The Second Diesel Spotter's Guide.* Milwaukee, Wis.: Kalmbach Publishing, 1973.

Reck, Franklin M. *On Time.* Electro-Motive Division of General Motors, 1948.

———. *The Dilworth Story.* New York: McGraw-Hill, 1954.

Rose, Joseph R. *American Wartime Transportation.* New York: Crowell, 1953.

Saunders, Richard Jr. *The Railroad Mergers and the Coming of Conrail.* Westport, Conn.: Greenwood Press, 1978.

———. *Merging Lines: American Railroads 1900–1970, 2nd Ed.* DeKalb, Ill.: Northern Illinois University Press, 2001.

Schneider, Paul D. *GM's Geeps: The General Purpose Diesel.* Waukesha, Wis.: Kalmbach Publishing, 2001.

Schrenk, Lorenz P., and Robert L. Frey. *Northern Pacific Diesel Era 1945–1970.* San Marino, Calif.: Golden West, 1988.

Shaughnessy, Jim. *Delaware & Hudson*. Berkeley, Calif.: Howell-North, 1967.

Signor, John R. *Tehachapi*. San Marino, Calif.: Golden West, 1983.

———. *Donner Pass: Southern Pacific's Sierra Crossing*. San Marino, Calif.: Golden West, 1985.

Solomon, Brian. *The American Diesel Locomotive*. Osceola, Wis.: MBI Publishing, 2000.

———. *Locomotive*. St. Paul, Minn.: MBI Publishing, 2001.

———. *Railway Masterpieces: Celebrating the World's Greatest Trains, Stations, and Feats of Engineering*. Iola, Wis.: Krause, 2002.

———. *GE Locomotives*. St. Paul, Minn.: MBI Publishing Company, 2003.

———. *Burlington Northern Santa Fe Railway*. St. Paul, Minn.: MBI Publishing Company, 2005.

———. *CSX*. St. Paul, Minn.: MBI Publishing, 2005.

———. *EMD Early Road Switchers: GP7–GP20 Locomotives*. North Branch, Minn.: Specialty Press, 2005.

———. *EMD F-Unit Locomotives*. North Branch, Minn.: Specialty Press, 2005.

———. *EMD Locomotives*. St. Paul, Minn.: MBI Publishing, 2006.

———. *Alco Locomotives*. Minneapolis: Voyageur Press, 2009.

Solomon, Brian, and Mike Schafer. *New York Central Railroad*. Osceola, Wis.: MBI Publishing, 1999.

Staff, Virgil. *D-Day on the Western Pacific*. Glendale, Calif.: Interurban Press, 1982.

Staufer, Alvin F. *Pennsy Power III*. Medina, Ohio: A. F. Staufer, 1993.

Staufer, Alvin F., and Edward L. May. *New York Central's Later Power 1910–1968*. Medina, Ohio: A. F. Staufer, 1981.

Steinbrenner, Richard T. *The American Locomotive Company: A Centennial Remembrance*. Warren, N.J.: On Track Publishers, 2003.

Strapac, Joseph A. *Southern Pacific Motive Power Annual, 1971*. Burlingame, Calif.: Chatham Publishing, 1971.

———. *Southern Pacific Review, 1981*. Huntington Beach, Calif.: Pacific Coast Chapter of the Railway and Locomotive Historical Society, 1982.

———. *Southern Pacific Review, 1953–1985*. Huntington Beach, Calif.: Pacific Coast Chapter of the Railway and Locomotive Historical Society, 1986.

———. *Southern Pacific Historic Diesels, Vols. 3–10*. Huntington Beach, Calif., and Bellflower, Calif.: Shade Tree Books, 2003.

Withers, Paul K. *Conrail Motive Power Review 1986–1991*. Halifax, Pa.: Withers Publishing, 1992.

BROCHURES, RULEBOOKS, AND TIMETABLES

Central Vermont Railway. *Timetable 65, Northern and Southern Division*. 1965.

Electro-Motive Division. *Instruction Manual 234: Diesel Freight Locomotives*. La Grange, Ill.: General Motors, 1945.

———.*Operating Manual No. 2300*. La Grange, Ill.: General Motors, 1945(?).

———. *Model 567B Engine Maintenance Manual*. La Grange, Ill.: General Motors, 1948.

———. *Model F3 Operating Manual No. 2308B*. La Grange, Ill.: General Motors, 1948.

———.*600 HP & 1200 HP Switching Locomotive Operating Manual No. 2303*. La Grange, Ill.: General Motors, 1950.

———.*Diesel Locomotive Operating Manual No. 2312 for Model GP7 with Vapor Car Steam Generator, 2nd Ed*. La Grange, Ill.: General Motors, 1950.

———. *Model GP7 Operating Manual No. 2312*. La Grange, Ill.: General Motors, 1950.

Electro-Motive Division. *Model F7 Operating Manual No. 2310*. La Grange, Ill.: General Motors, 1951.

———.*Diesel Locomotive Operating Manual No. 2318 for Model GP9, 3rd Ed*. La Grange, Ill.: General Motors, 1957.

———.*Replacement Parts Catalog No. 301. Diesel Electro-Motive Division Replacement Parts Catalog No. 301. Diesel Engines*. La Grange, Ill.: General Motors, 1970.

———. *SD45 Operator's Manual*. La Grange, Ill.: General Motors, 1977.

GE Diesel Engines: Power for Progress. Erie, Pa.: General Electric, 1988.

A New Generation for Increased Productivity. Erie, Pa.: General Electric, 1984.

On the Road Trouble-Shooting. TS-4 GP7. La Grange, Ill.: General Motors, 1952.

BROCHURES, RULEBOOKS, AND TIMETABLES (*cont.*)

Operating Manual Model RS-3. American Locomotive Company, General Electric Company, 1951.

Seaboard Coast Line. *Instructions and Information Pertaining to Diesel Electric Engines*. Seaboard Coast Line, 1972.

Training Manual for General Motors Electro-Motive Division Model F9 Operating Manual No. 2315. La Grange, Ill.: General Motors, 1954.

PERIODICALS

Baldwin Locomotives. Philadelphia, Pa. [no longer published]

CTC Board, Ferndale. Wash.

Diesel Era. Halifax, Pa.

Diesel Railway Traction (supplement to *Railway Gazette*, U.K., merged into *Railway Gazette*).

Extra 2200 South. Cincinnati, Ohio.

Jane's World Railways. London.

Modern Railways. Surrey, U.K.

Official Guide to the Railways. New York.

Pacific RailNews. Waukesha, Wis. [no longer published]

Passenger Train Journal. Waukesha, Wis. [no longer published]

Railroad History (formerly *Railway and Locomotive Historical Society Bulletin*), Boston.

Railway and Locomotive Engineering [no longer published].

Railway Mechanical Engineer 1925–1952 [no longer published].

Railway Age. Chicago and New York.

Shoreliner. Grafton, Mass.

Trains Magazine. Waukesha, Wis.

Vintage Rails. Waukesha, Wis. [no longer published]